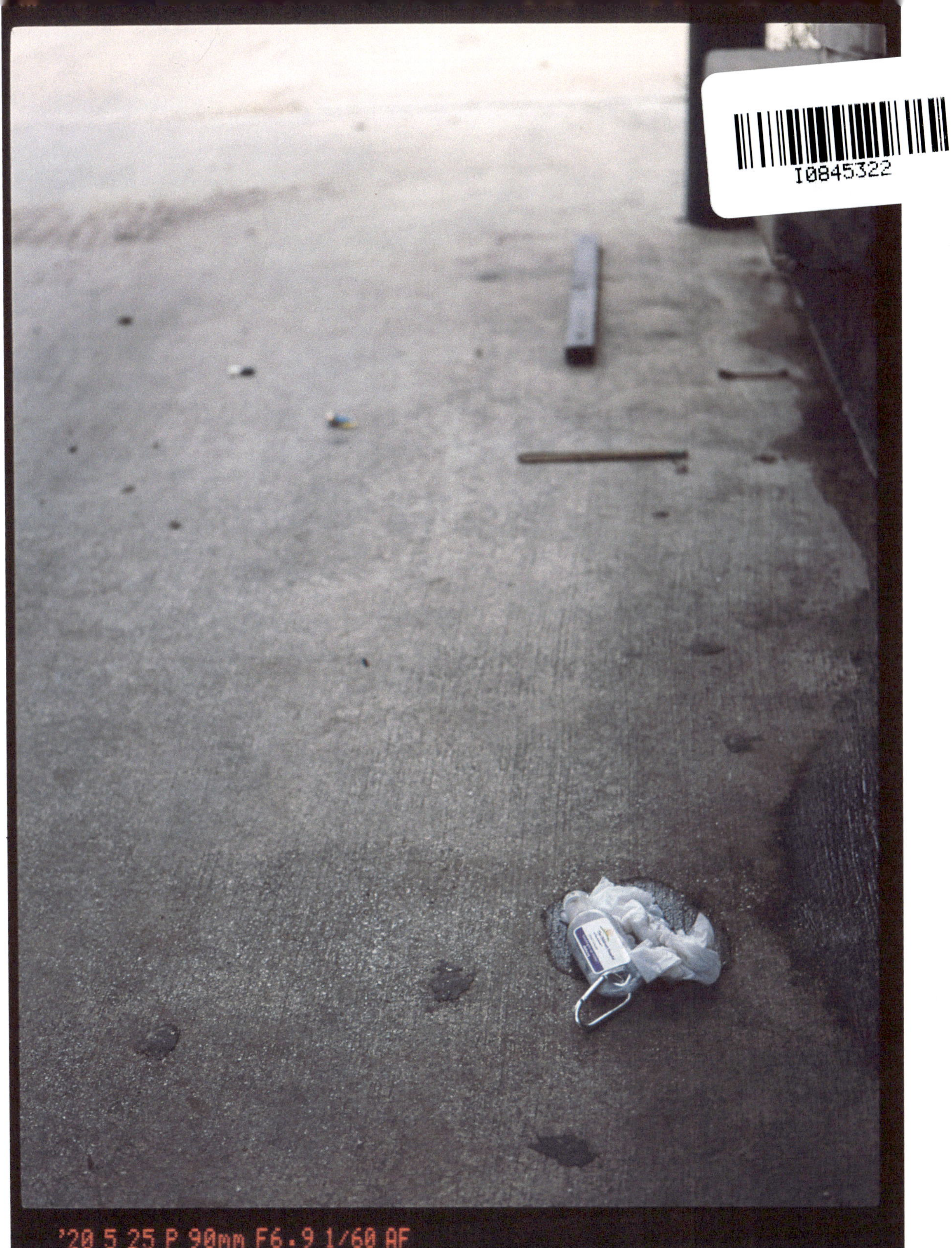
I0845322
'20 5 25 P 90mm F6.9 1/60 AF

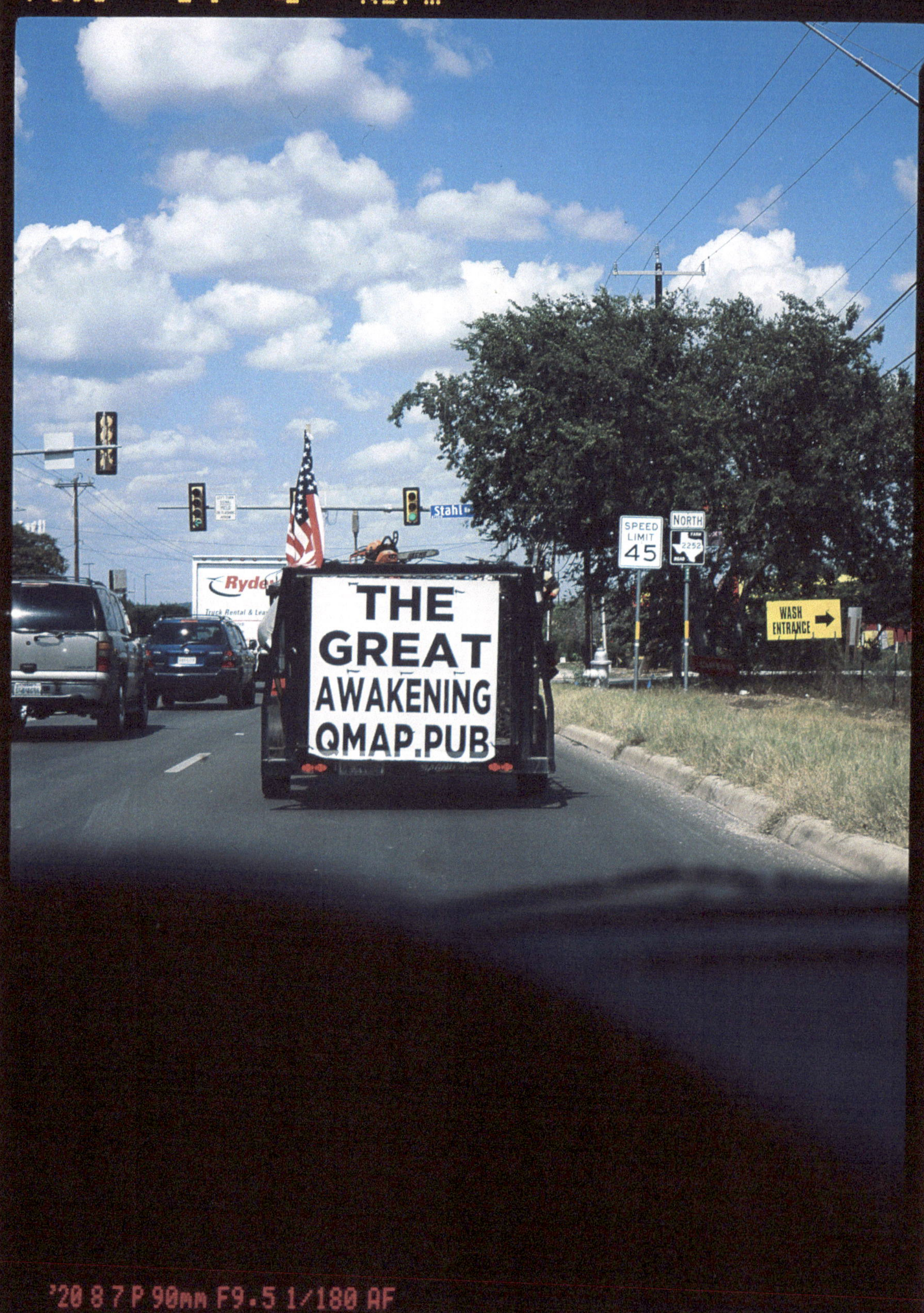
THE
GREAT
AWAKENING
QMAP.PUB
Ryder
Truck Rental & Leasing
Stahl
SPEED
LIMIT
45
NORTH
FARM
2252
WASH
ENTRANCE

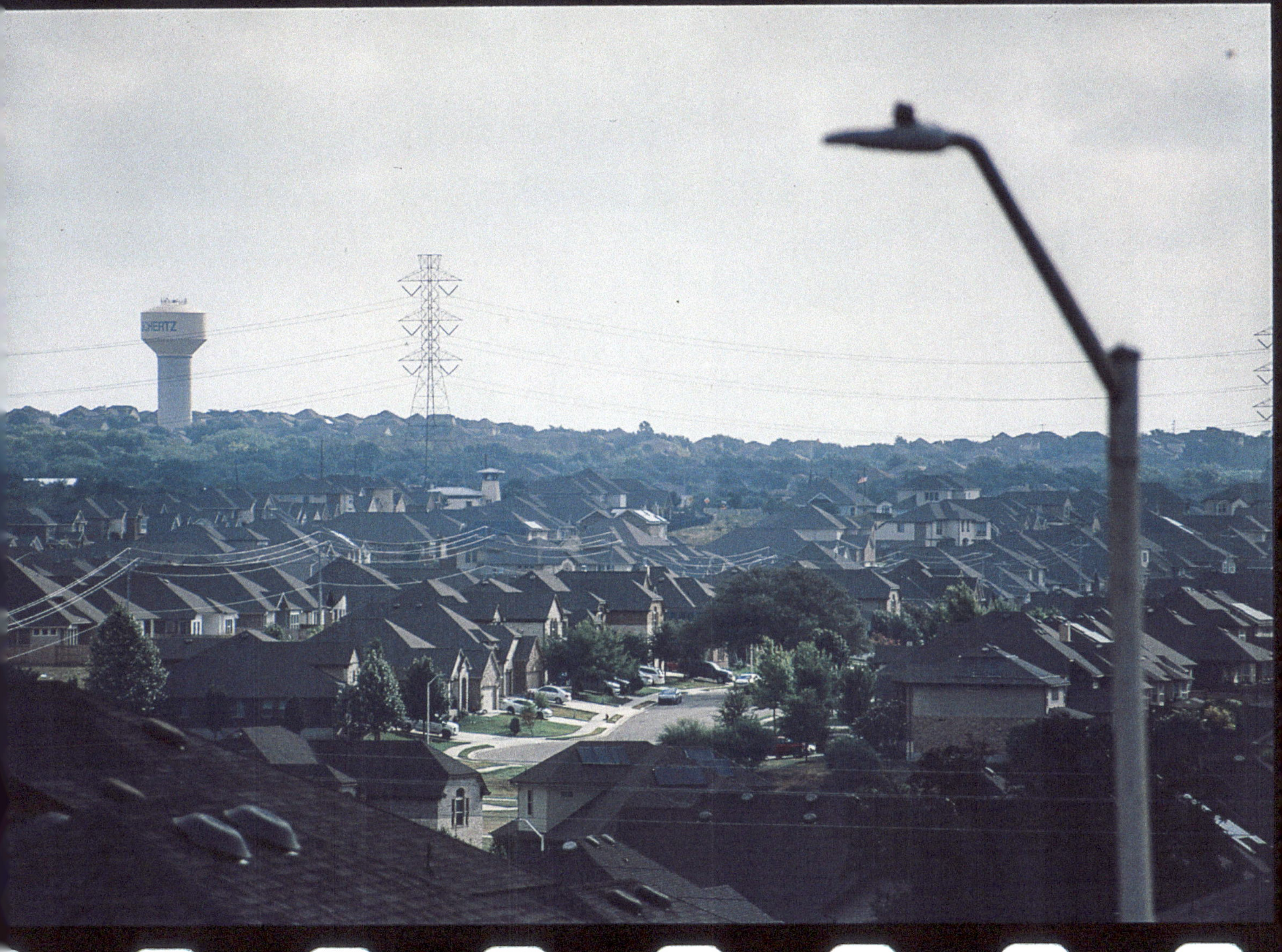

33
FUJI RDPⅢ
SCHERTZ
33
36 33A

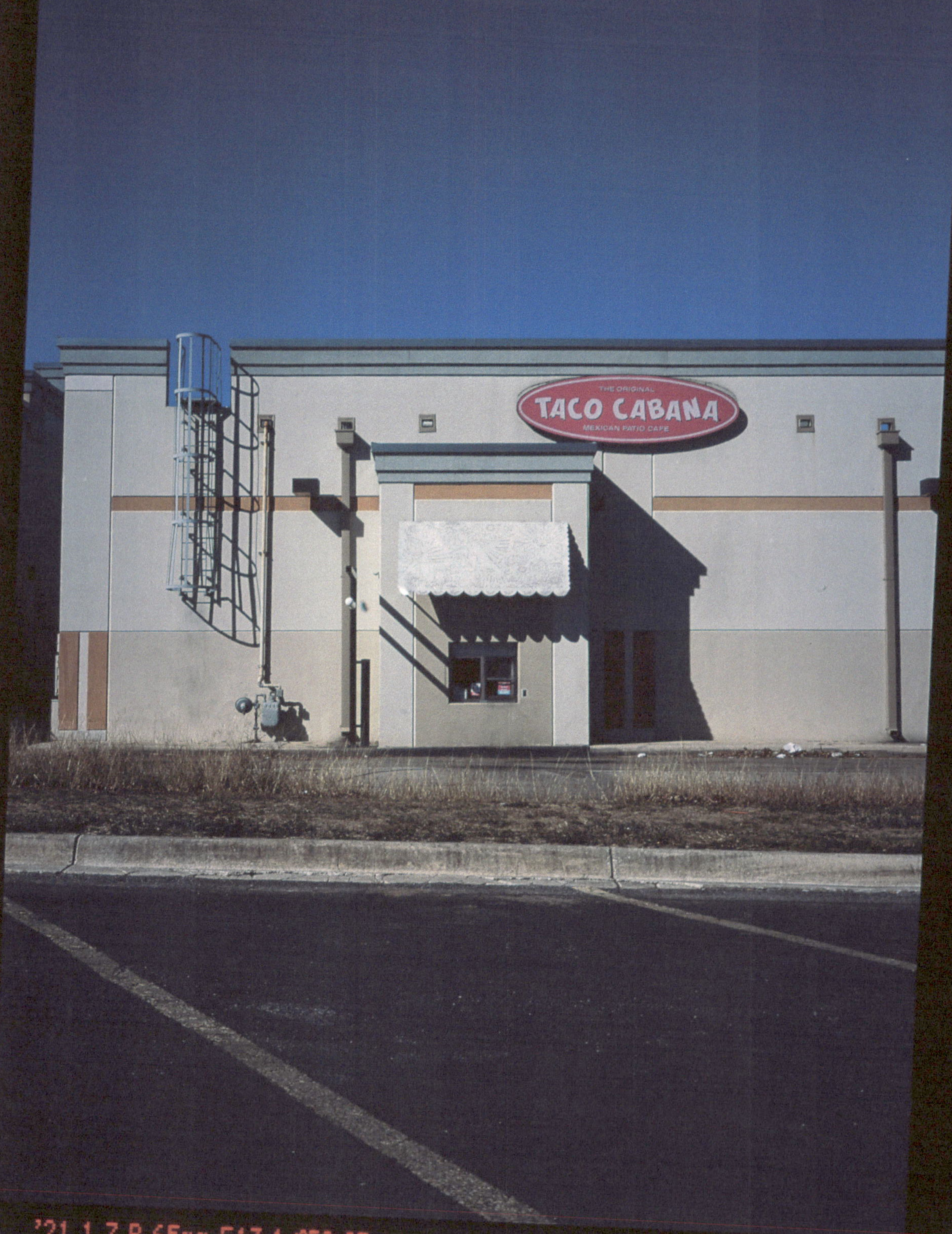
THE ORIGINAL
TACO CABANA
MEXICAN PATIO CAFE

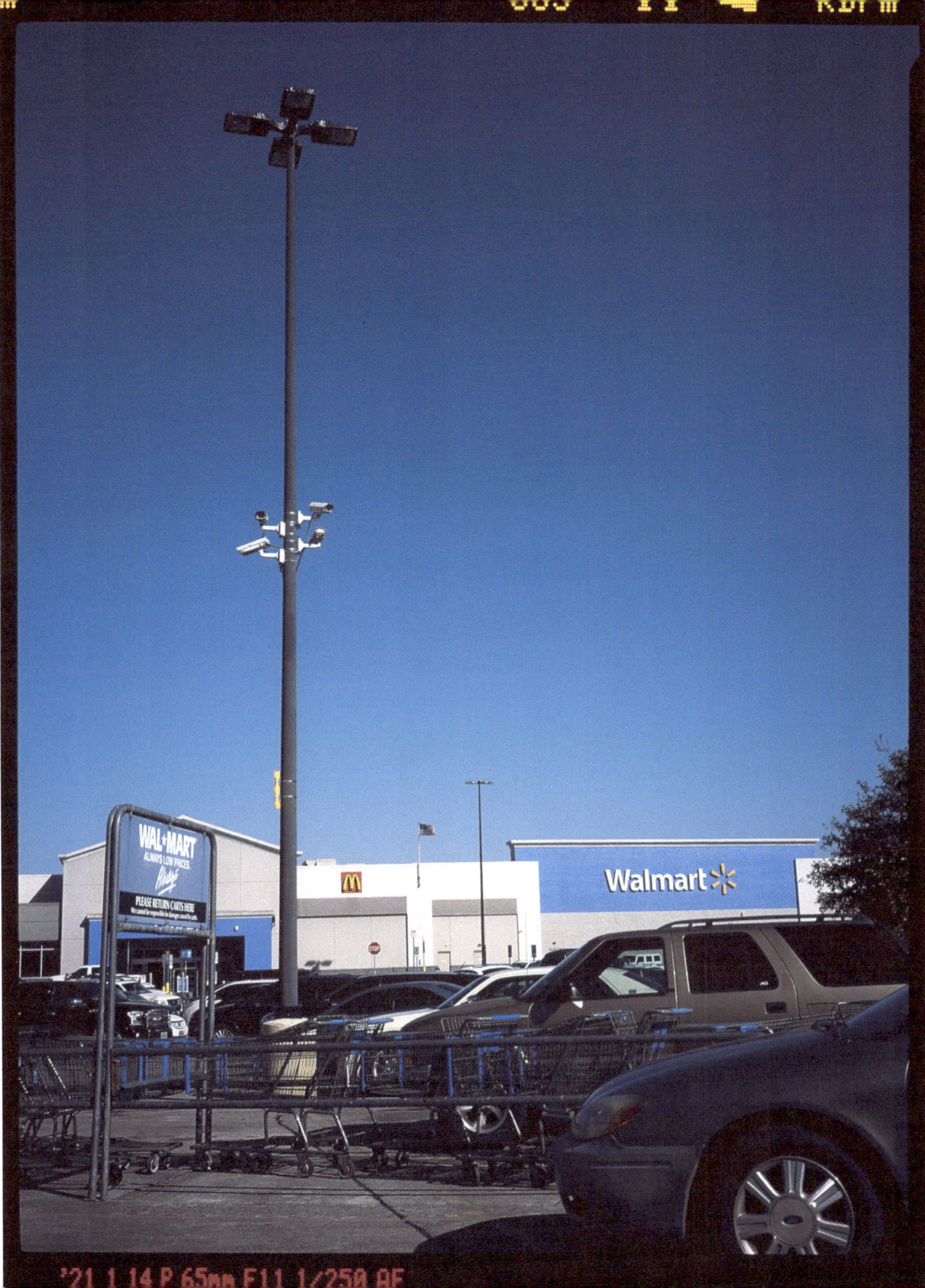

WAL★MART
ALWAYS LOW PRICES.
Always
PLEASE RETURN CARTS HERE
Walmart
STOP
'21 1 14 P 65mm F11 1/250 AE

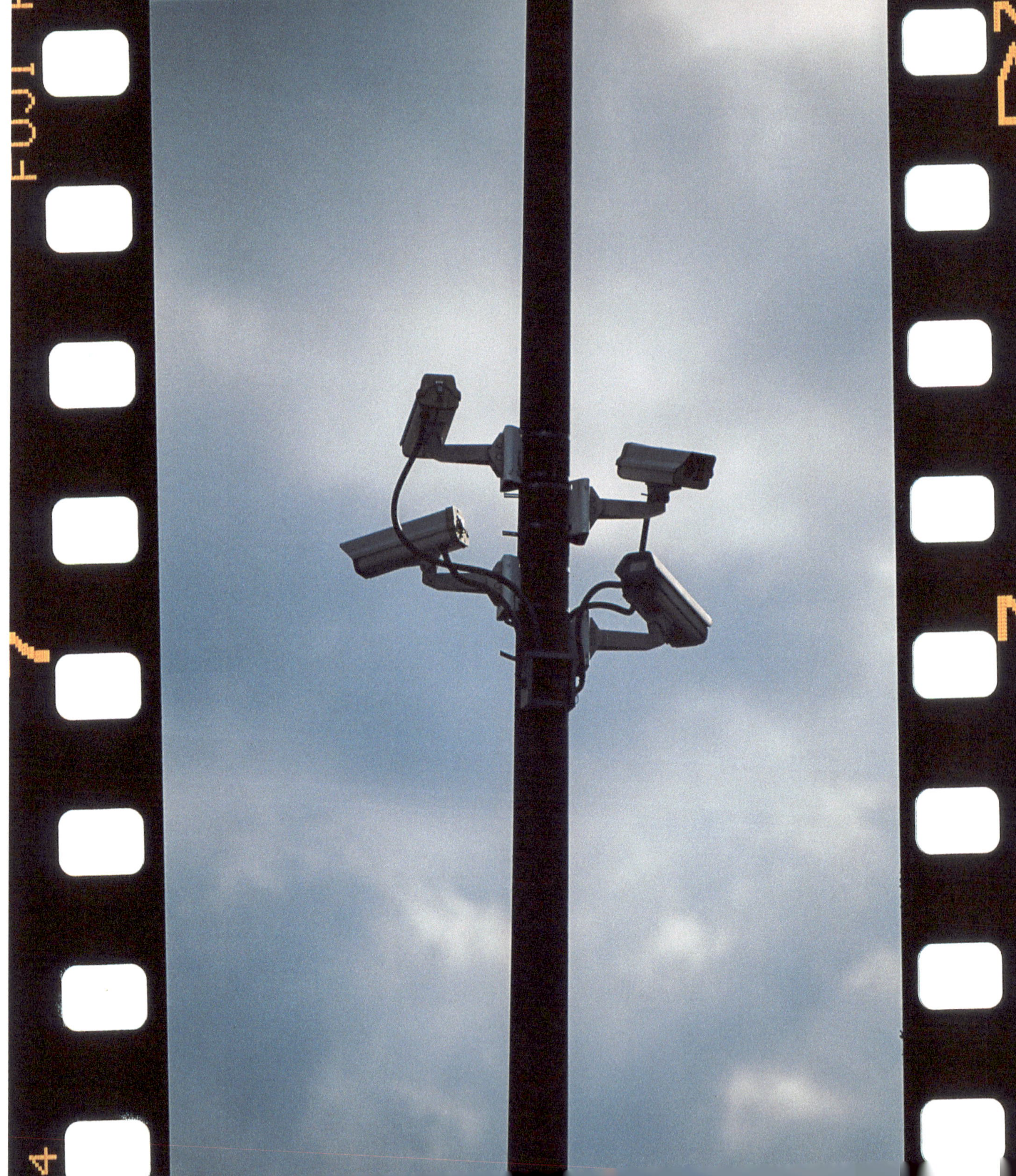

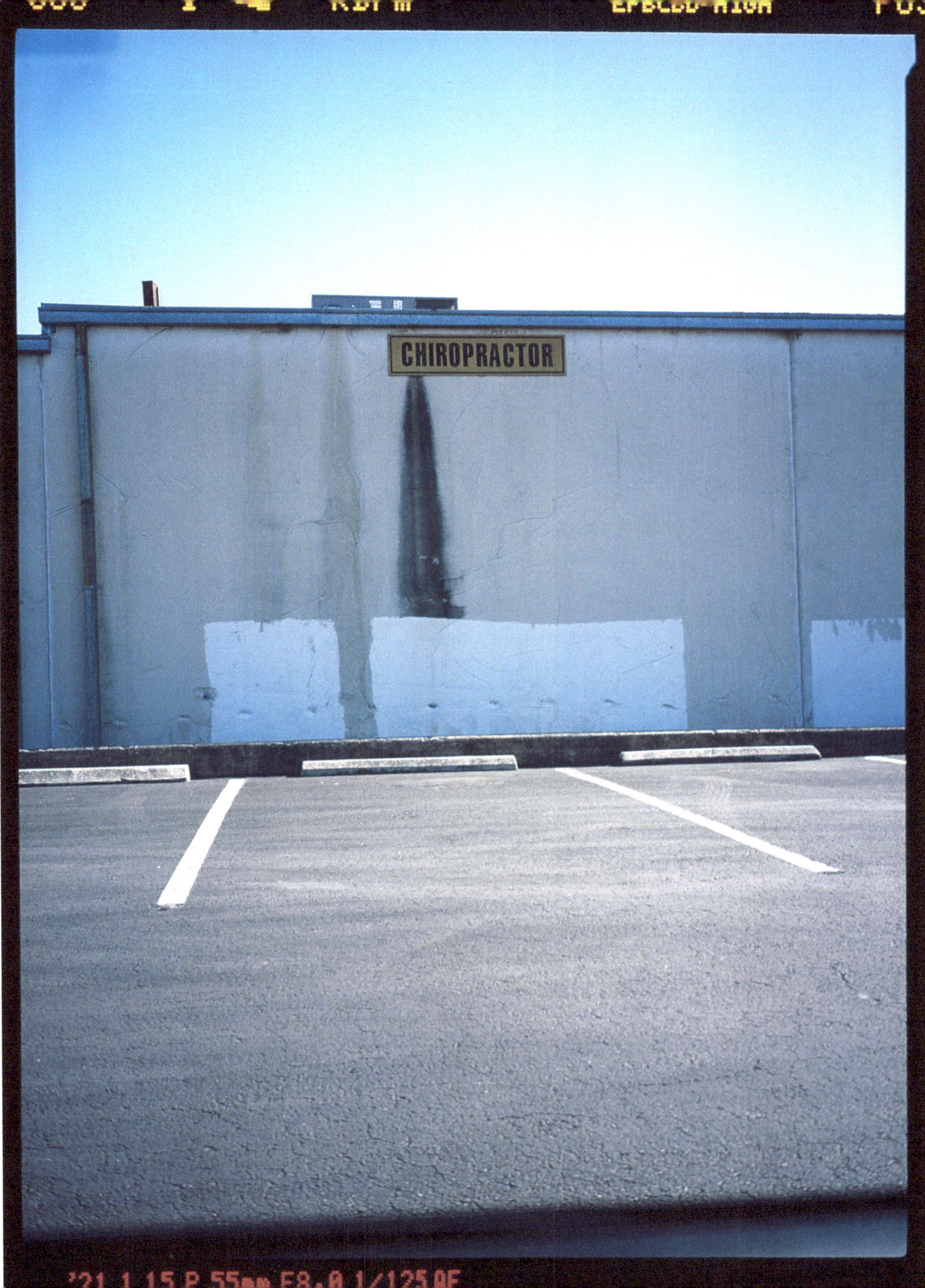
CHIROPRACTOR

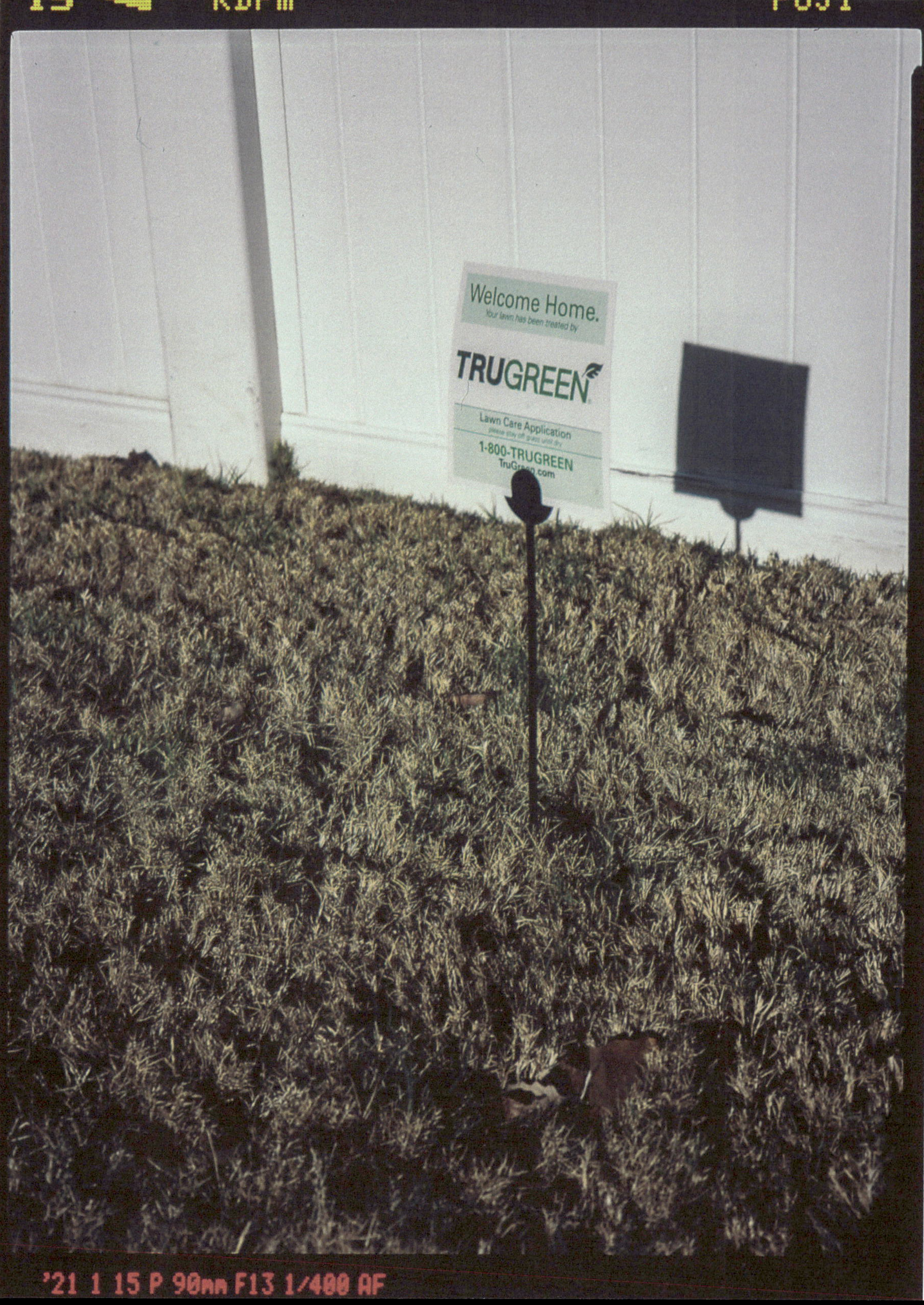
Welcome Home.
Your lawn has been treated by
TRUGREEN®
Lawn Care Application
please stay off grass until dry
1-800-TRUGREEN
TruGreen.com
'21 1 15 P 90mm F13 1/400 AF

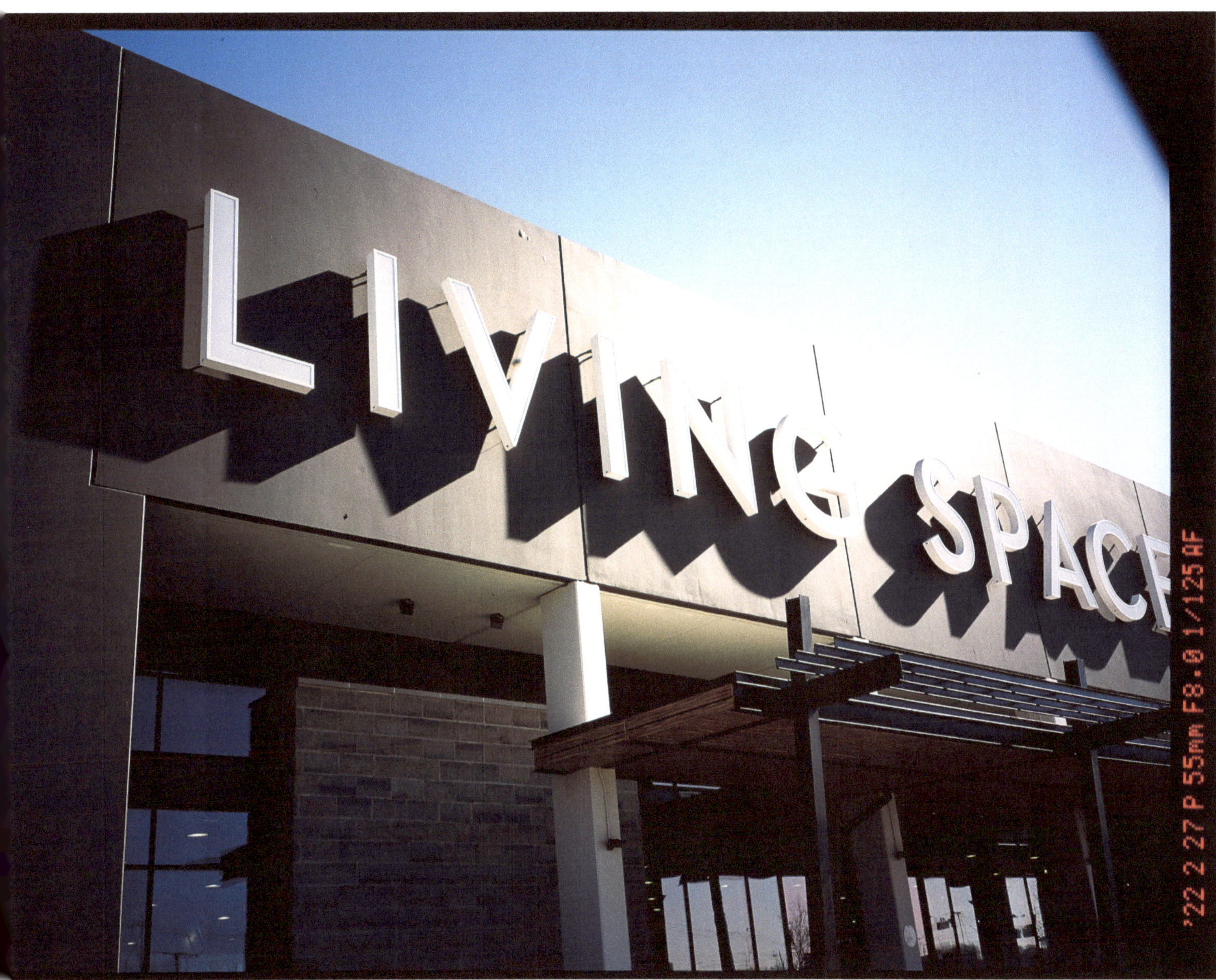

LIVING SPACE

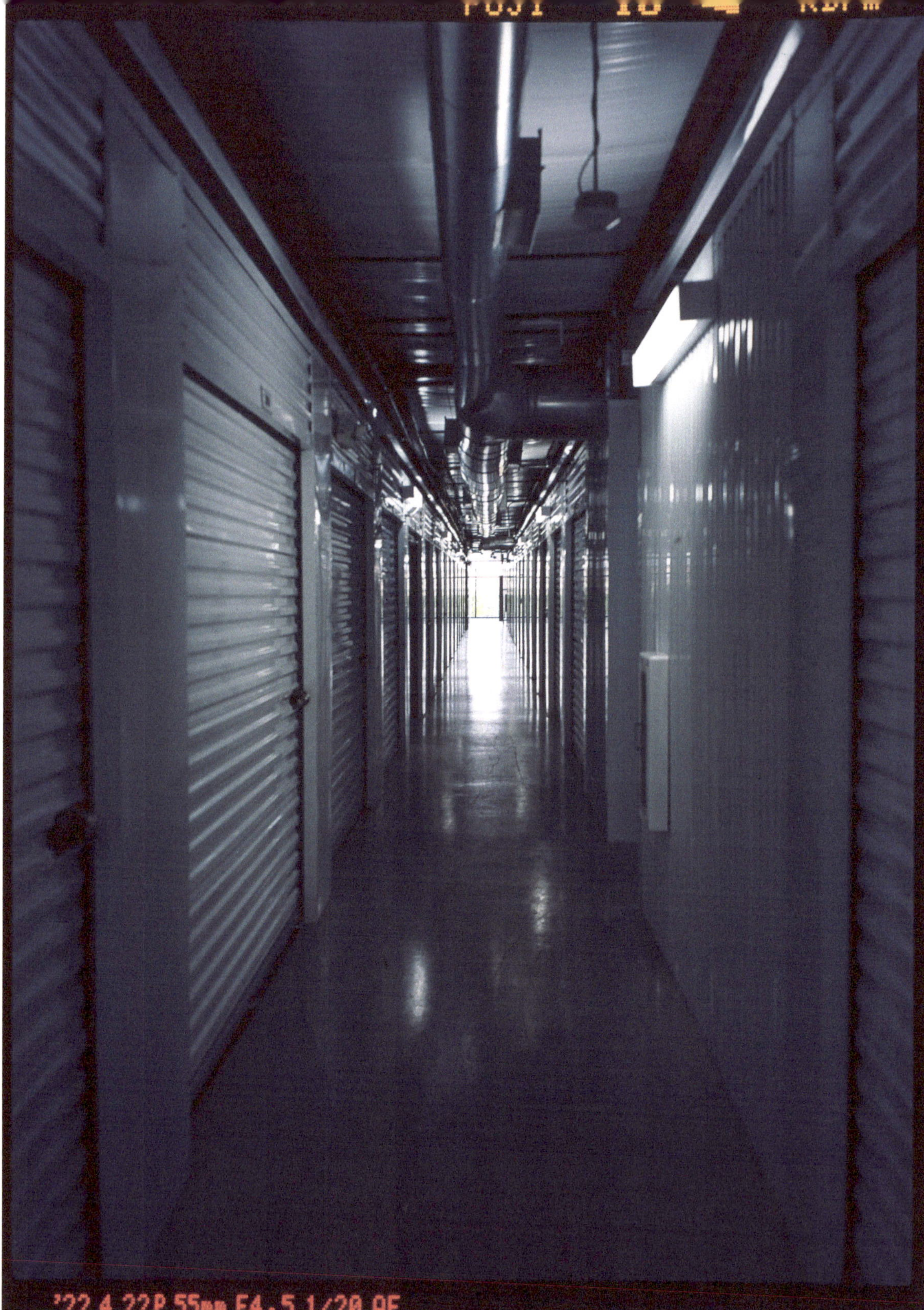

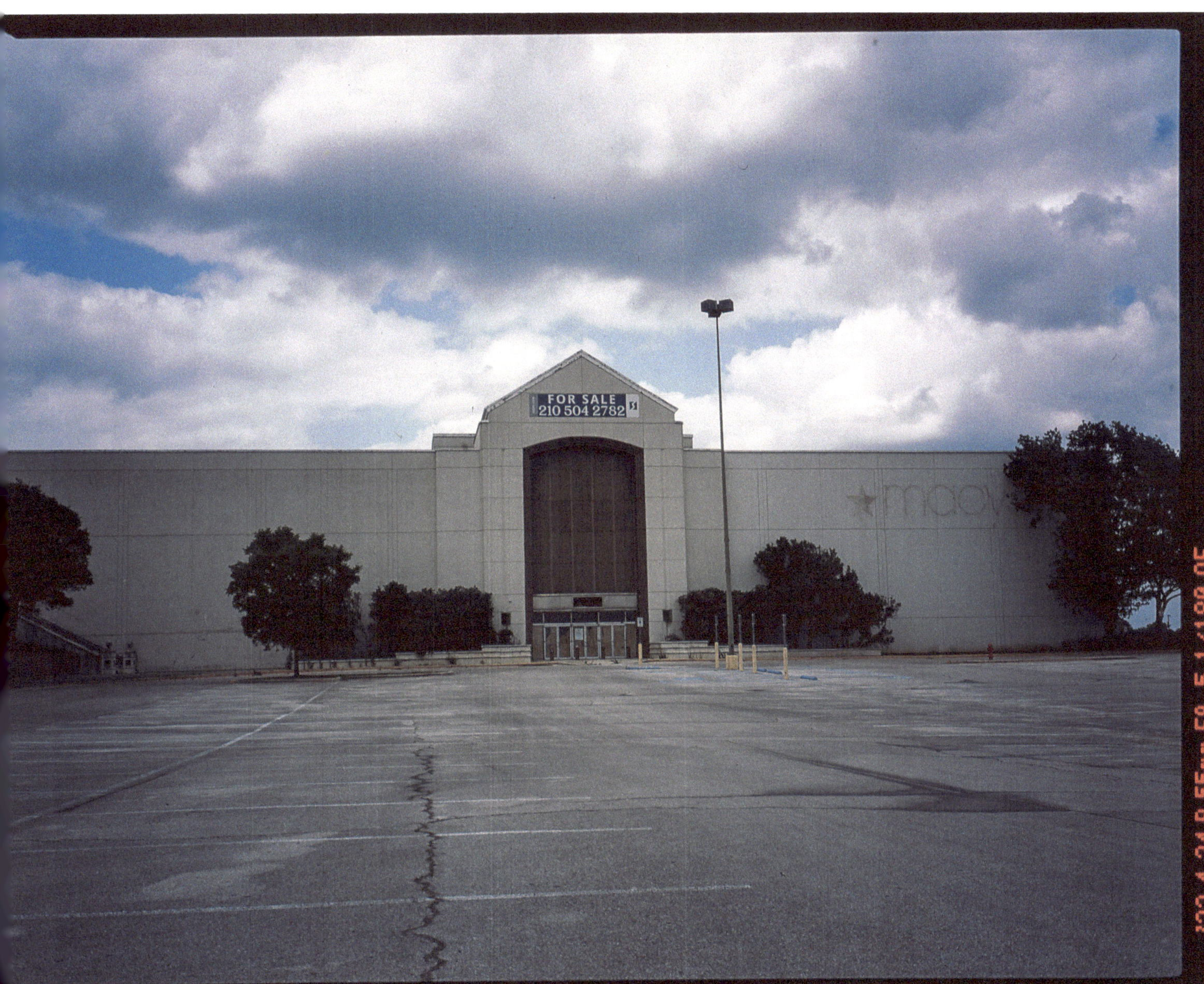

FOR SALE
210 504 2782

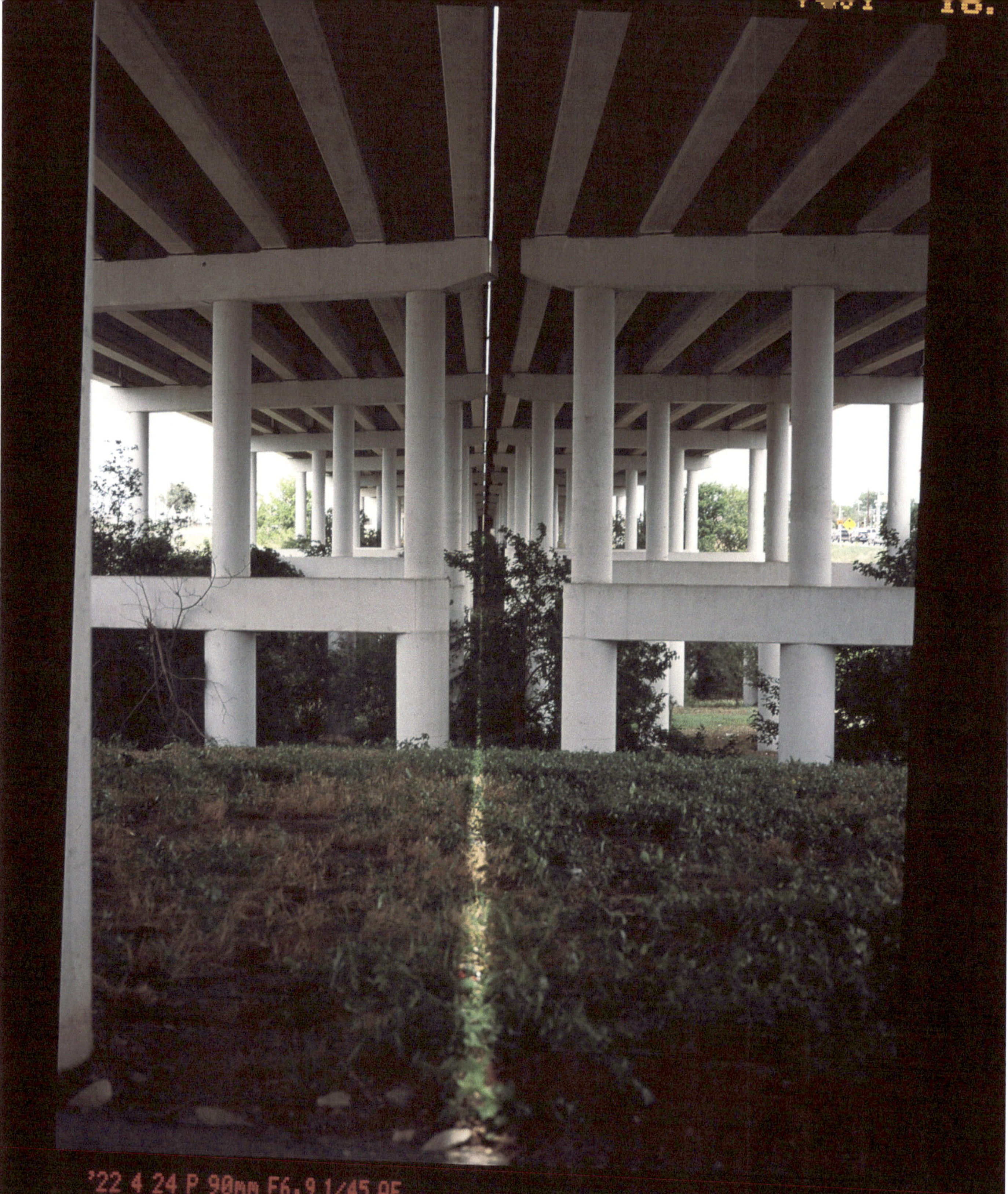
'22 4 24 P 90mm F6.9 1/45 AF

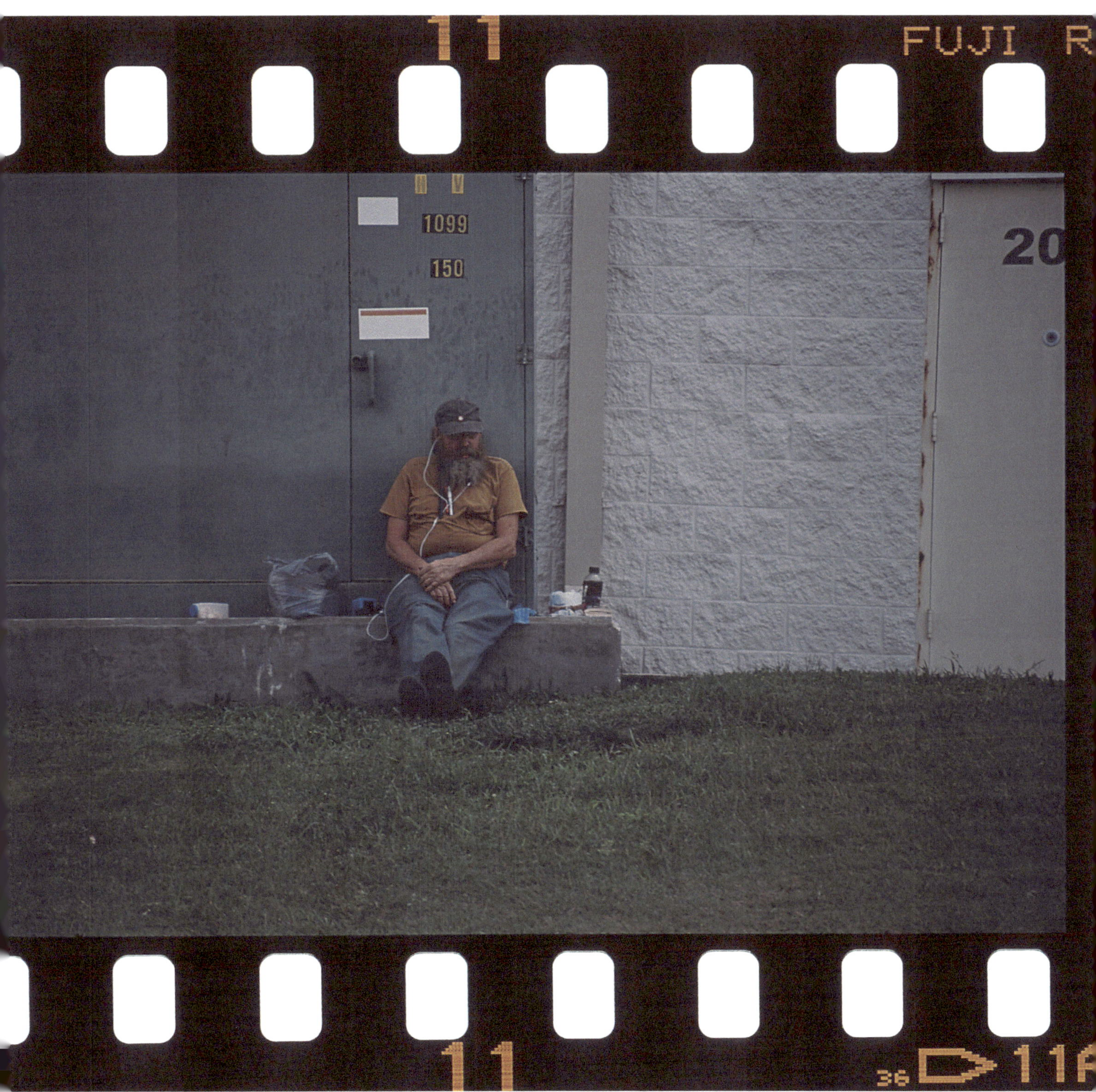

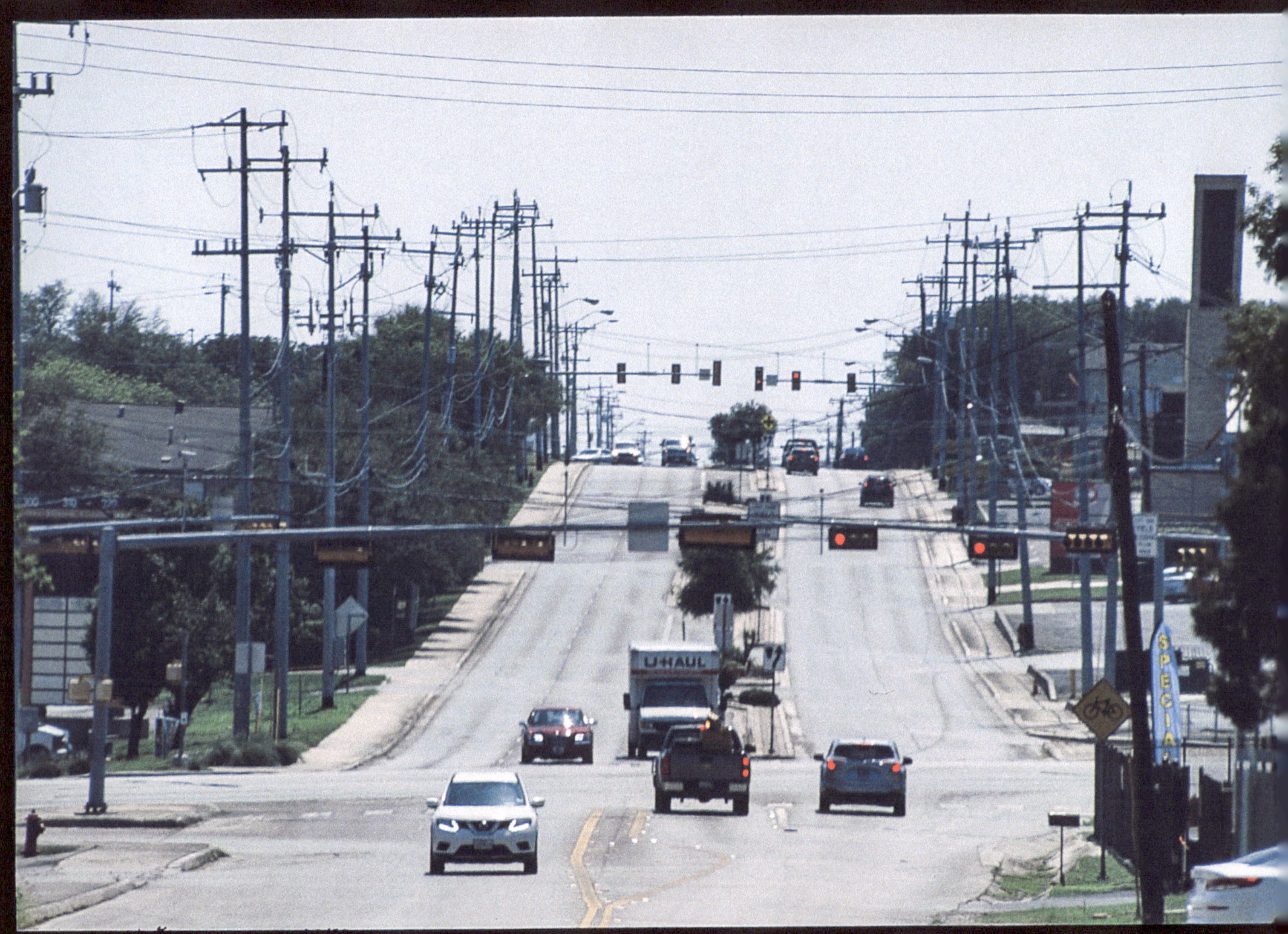

7
FUJI RDP
36 7A
7

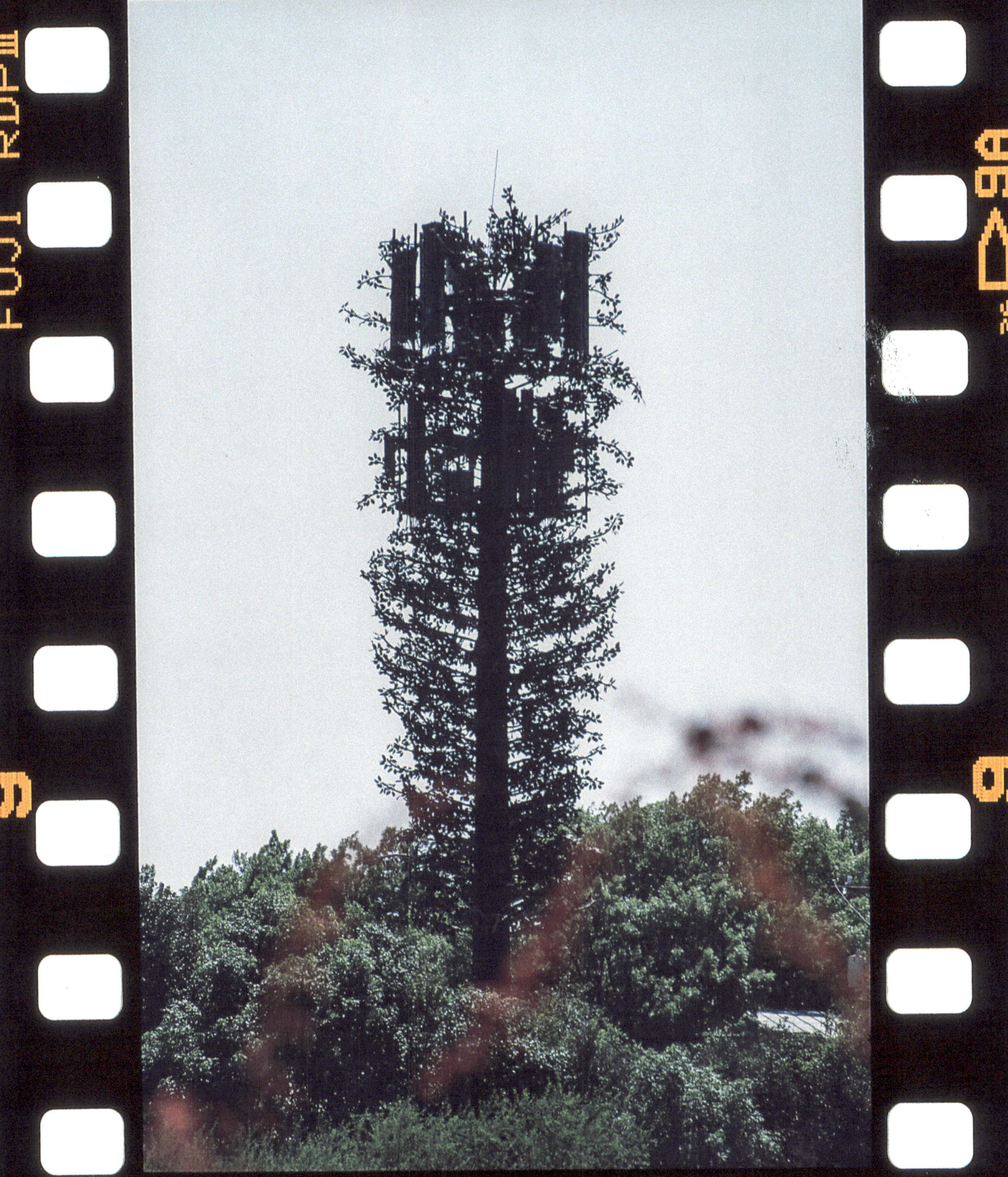

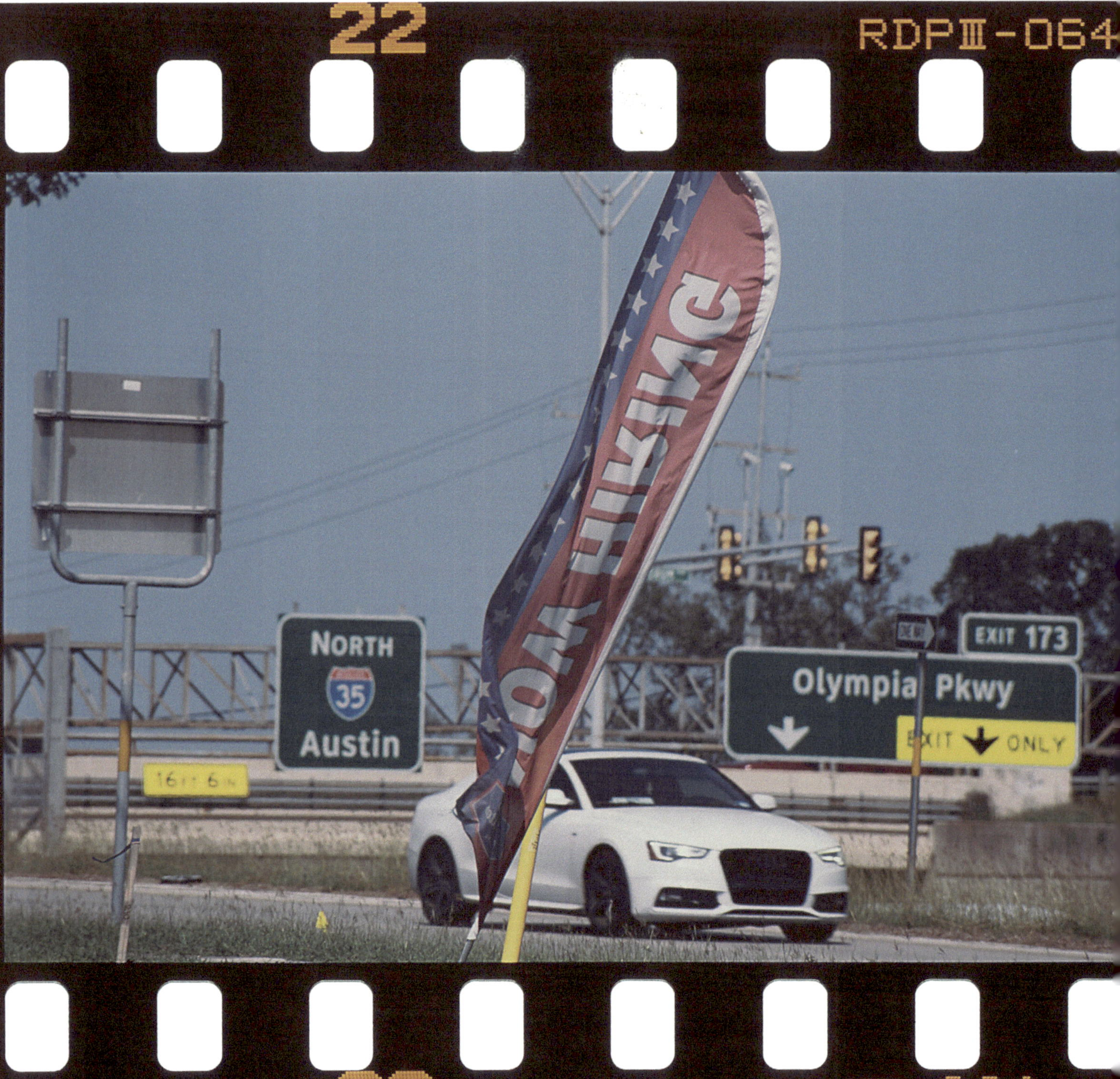
QUIT HIKING
NORTH
35
Austin
16 ft 6 in
EXIT 173
Olympia Pkwy
EXIT ONLY

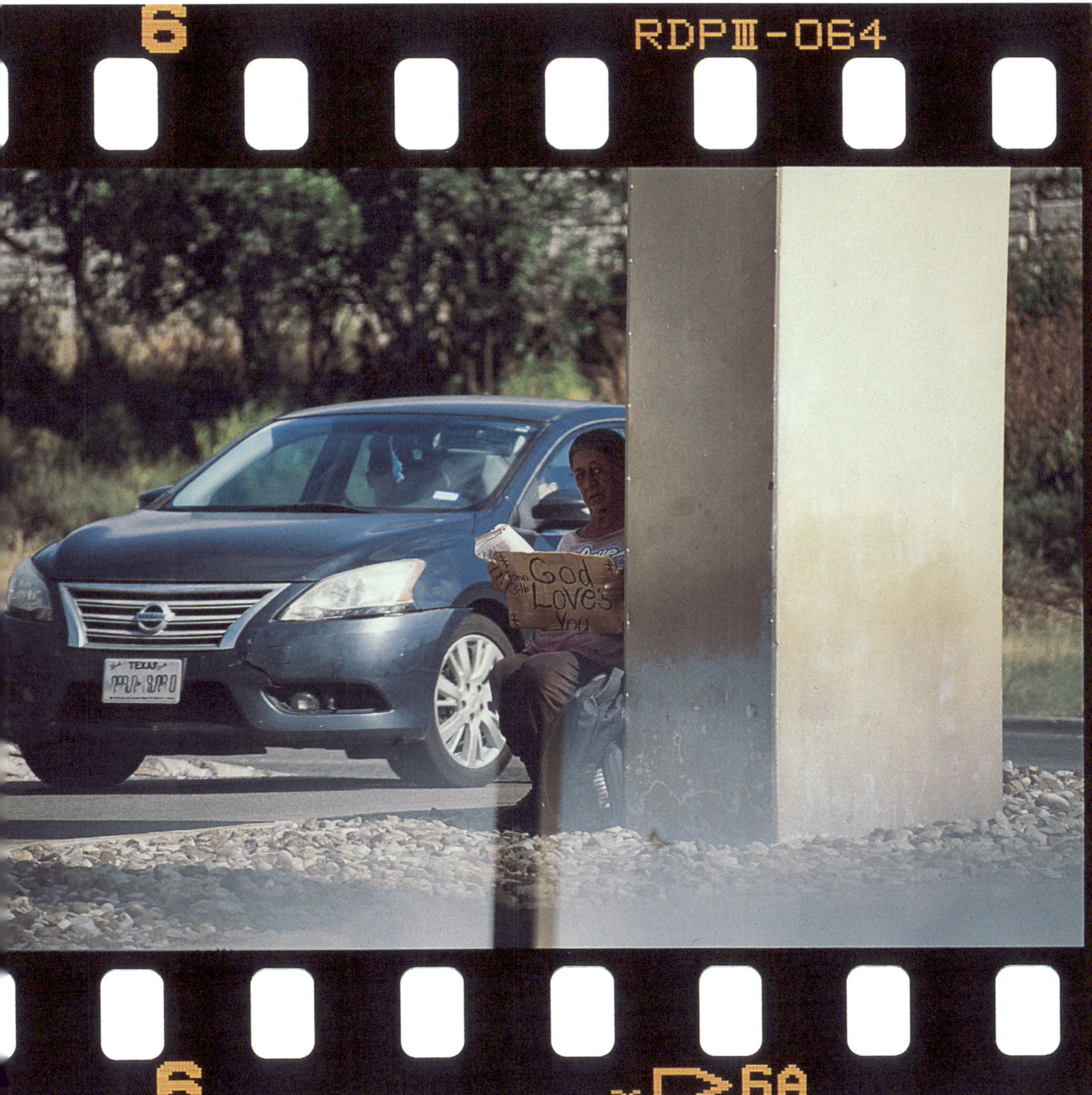
RDPⅢ-064
God
Love's
You
TEXAS
36

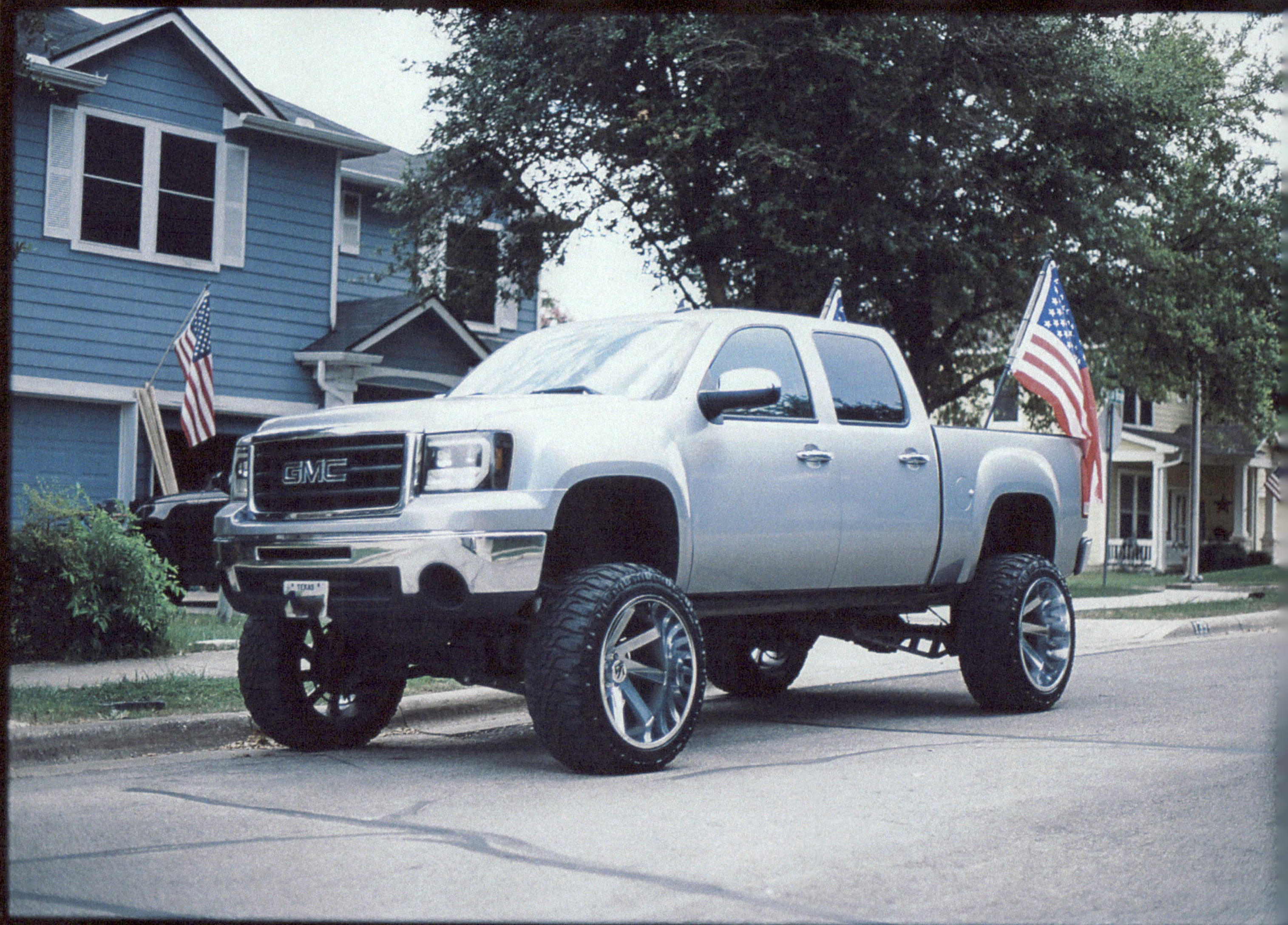
FUJI RDPⅢ
GMC
TEXAS
36 33A

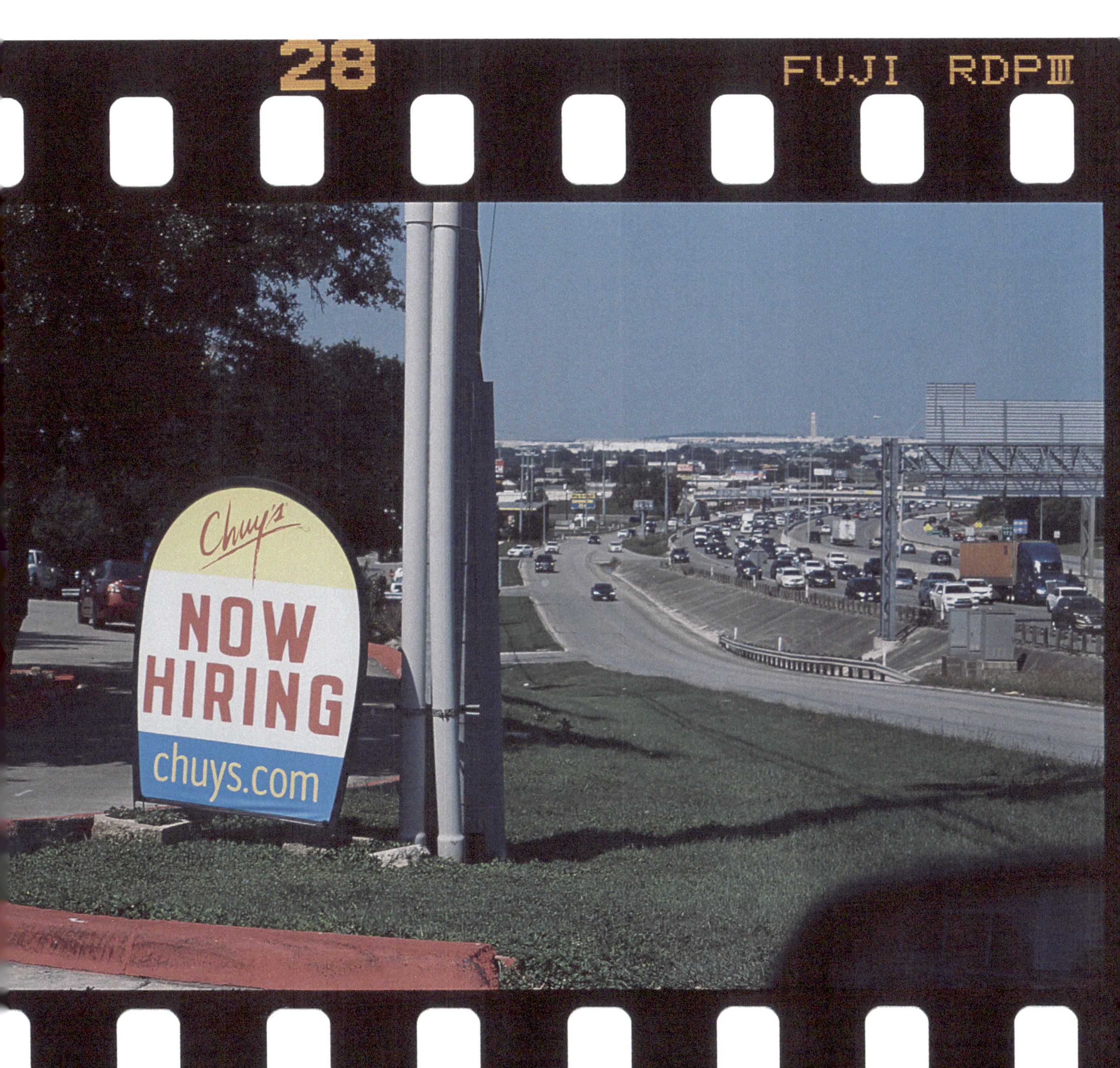
28
FUJI RDP III
Chuy's
NOW HIRING
chuys.com
28
36 28A

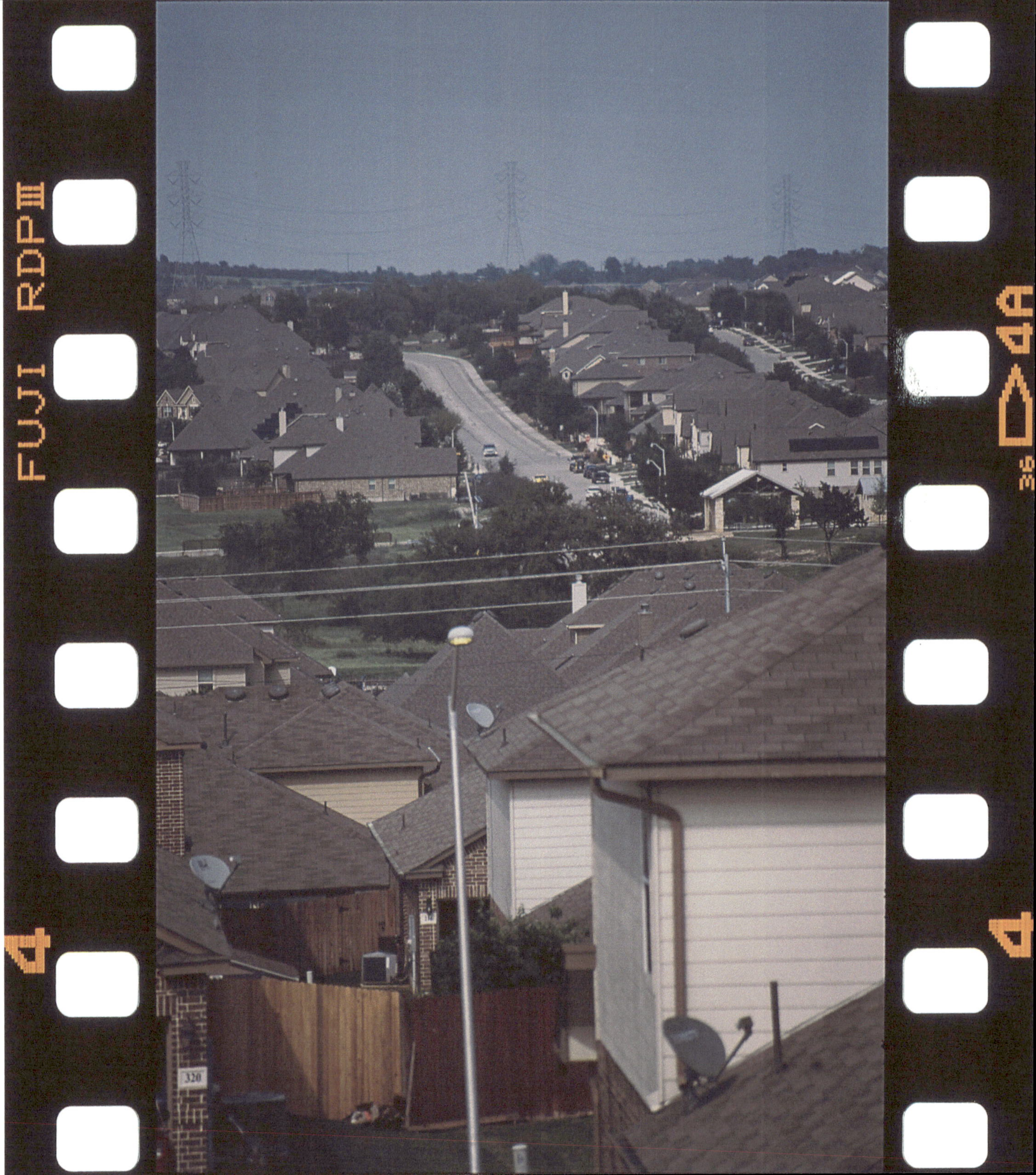

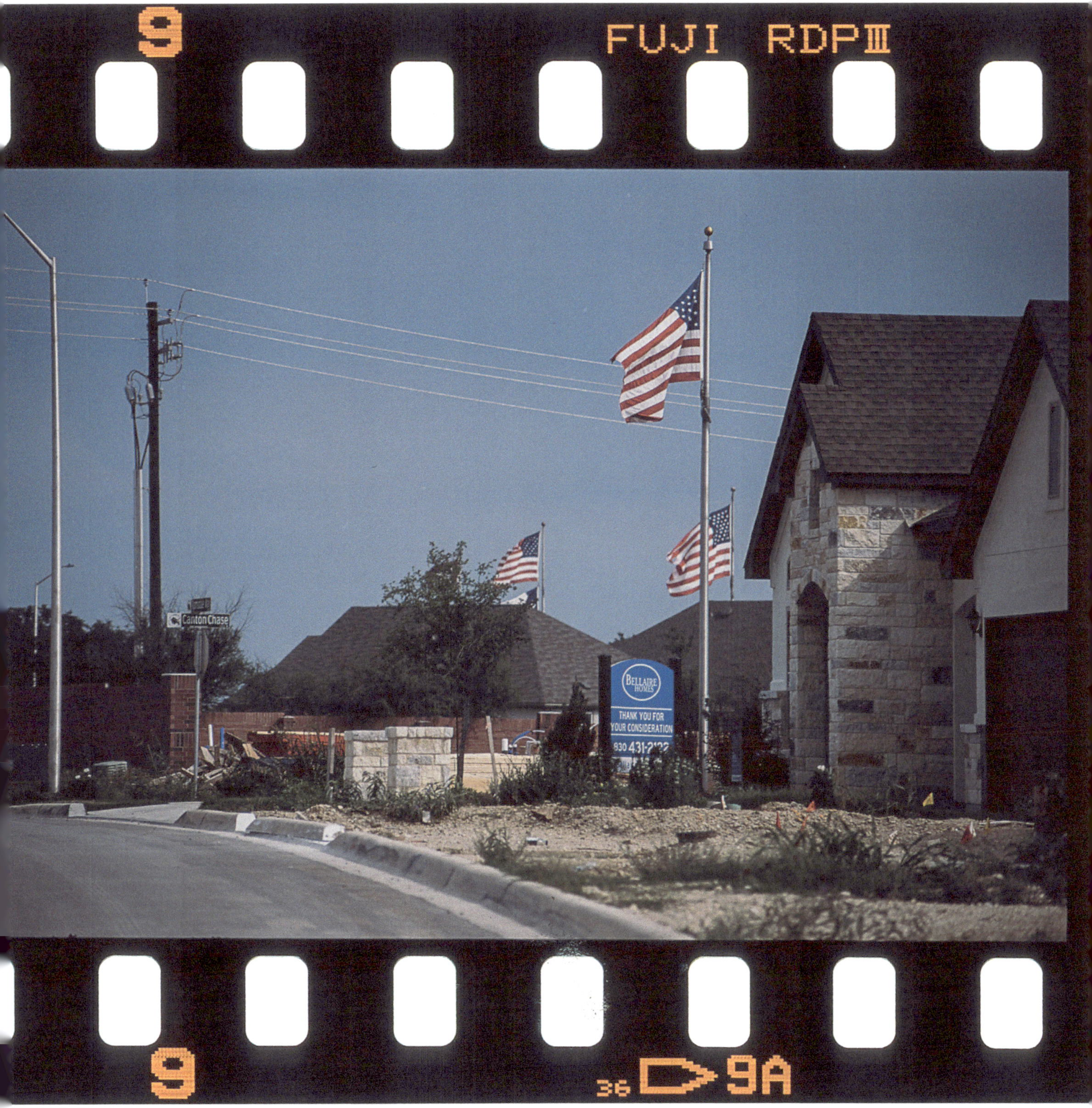

FUJI RDPⅢ
Canton Chase
BELLAIRE
HOMES
THANK YOU FOR
YOUR CONSIDERATION
830 431-2122
36 9A
9

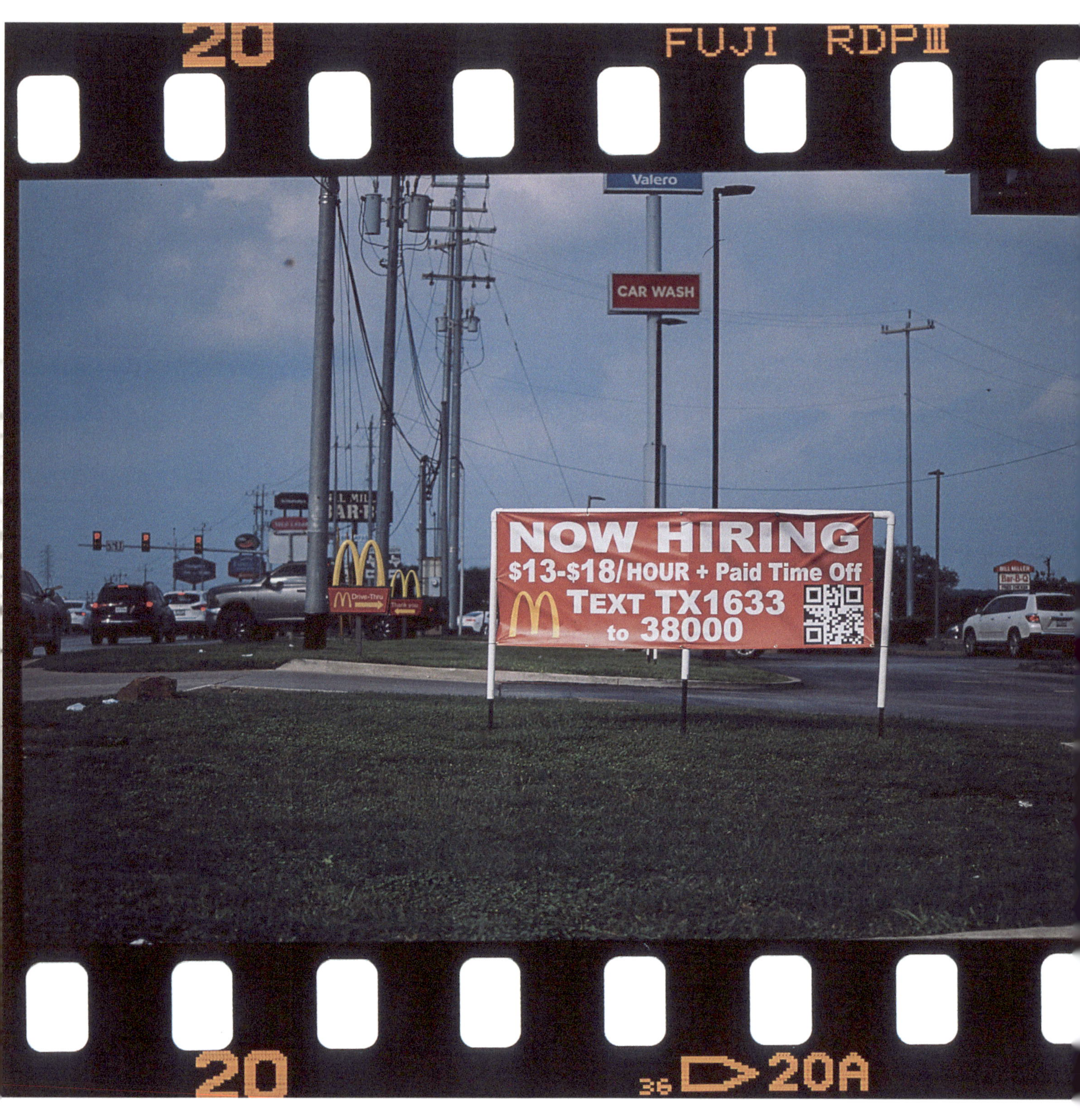
20
FUJI RDP III
Valero
CAR WASH
NOW HIRING
$13-$18/HOUR + Paid Time Off
TEXT TX1633
to 38000
Drive-Thru
Thank you
20
36
20A

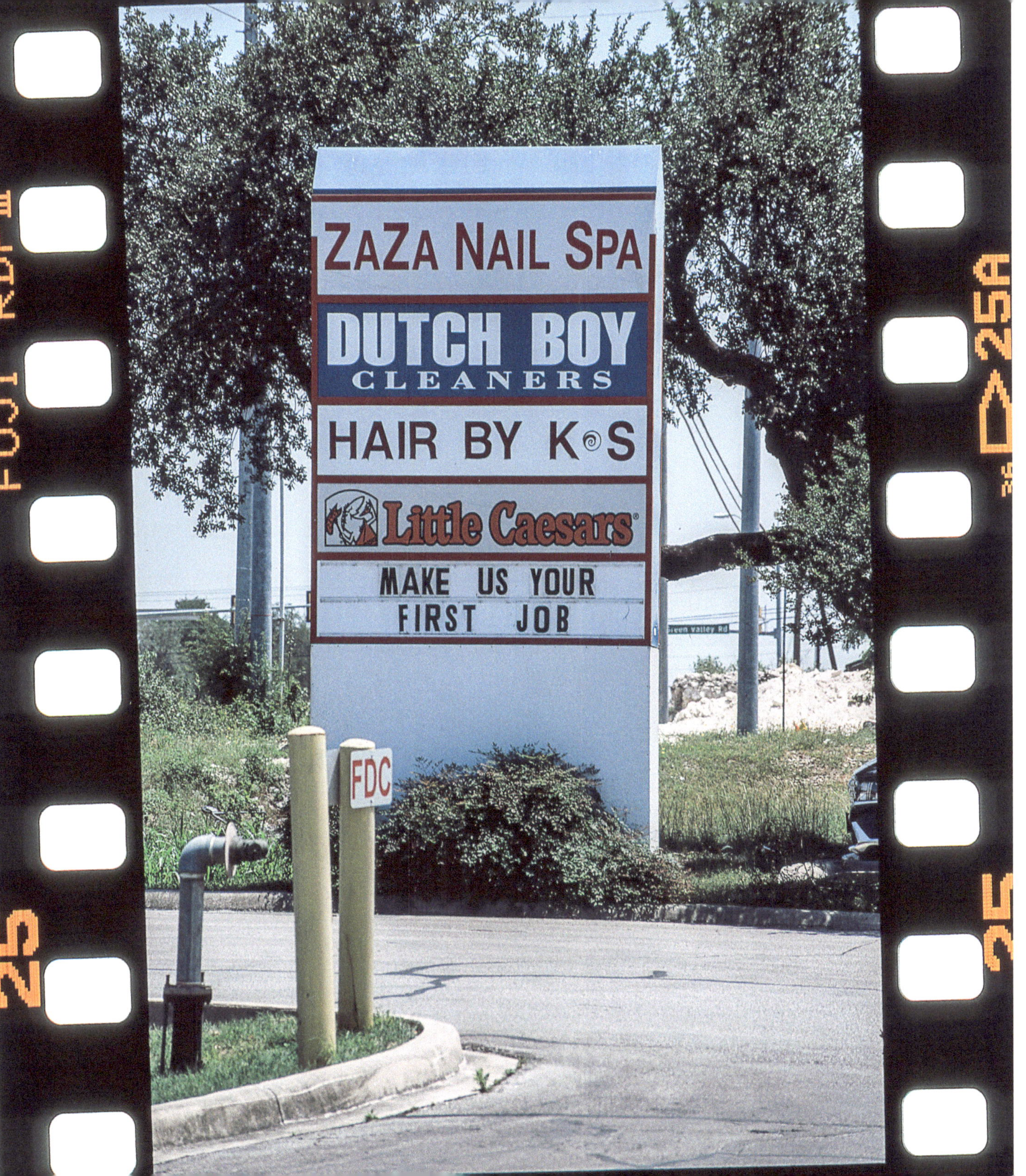
ZaZa Nail Spa
DUTCH BOY
CLEANERS
HAIR BY K·S
Little Caesars
MAKE US YOUR
FIRST JOB
FDC

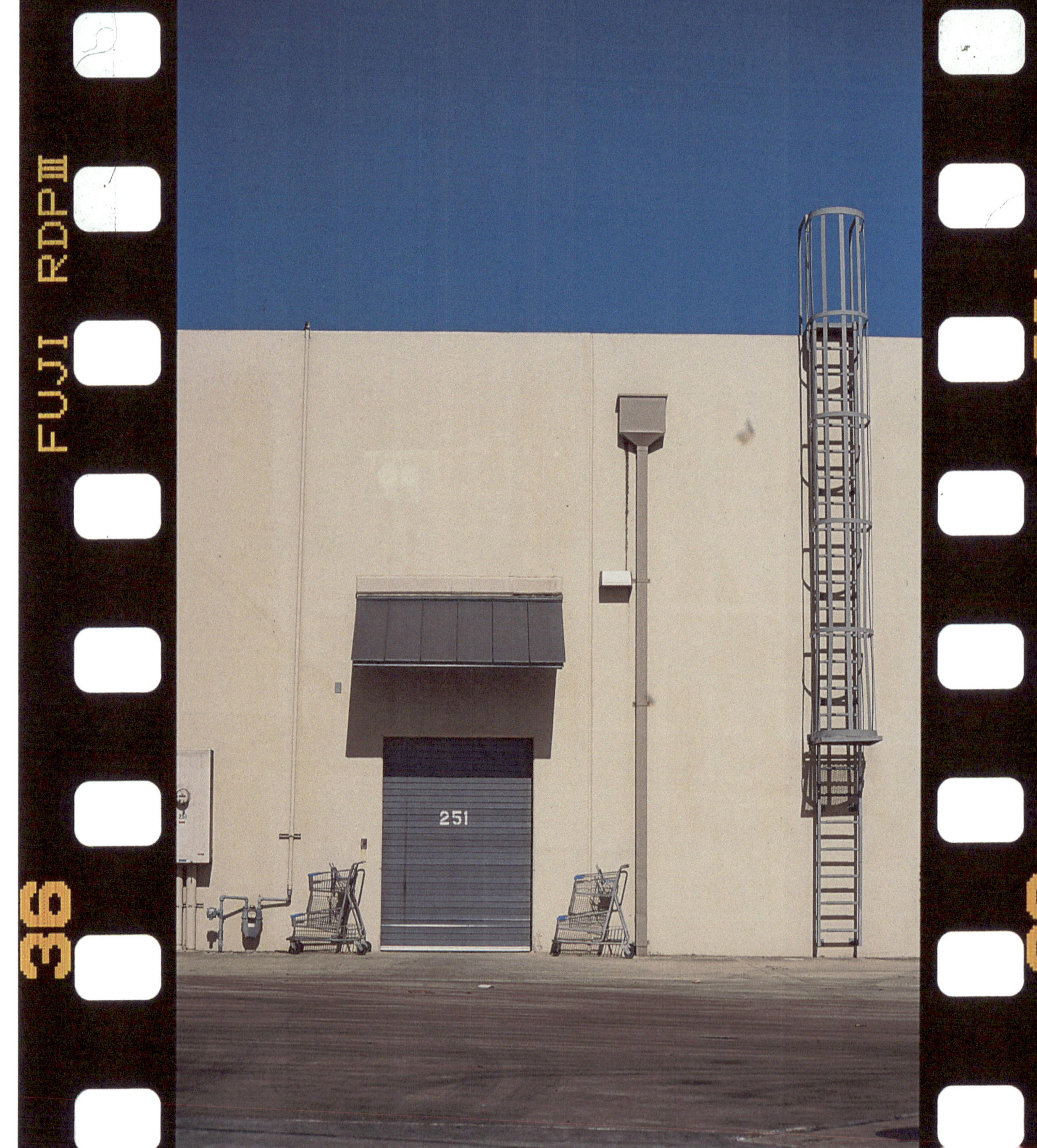

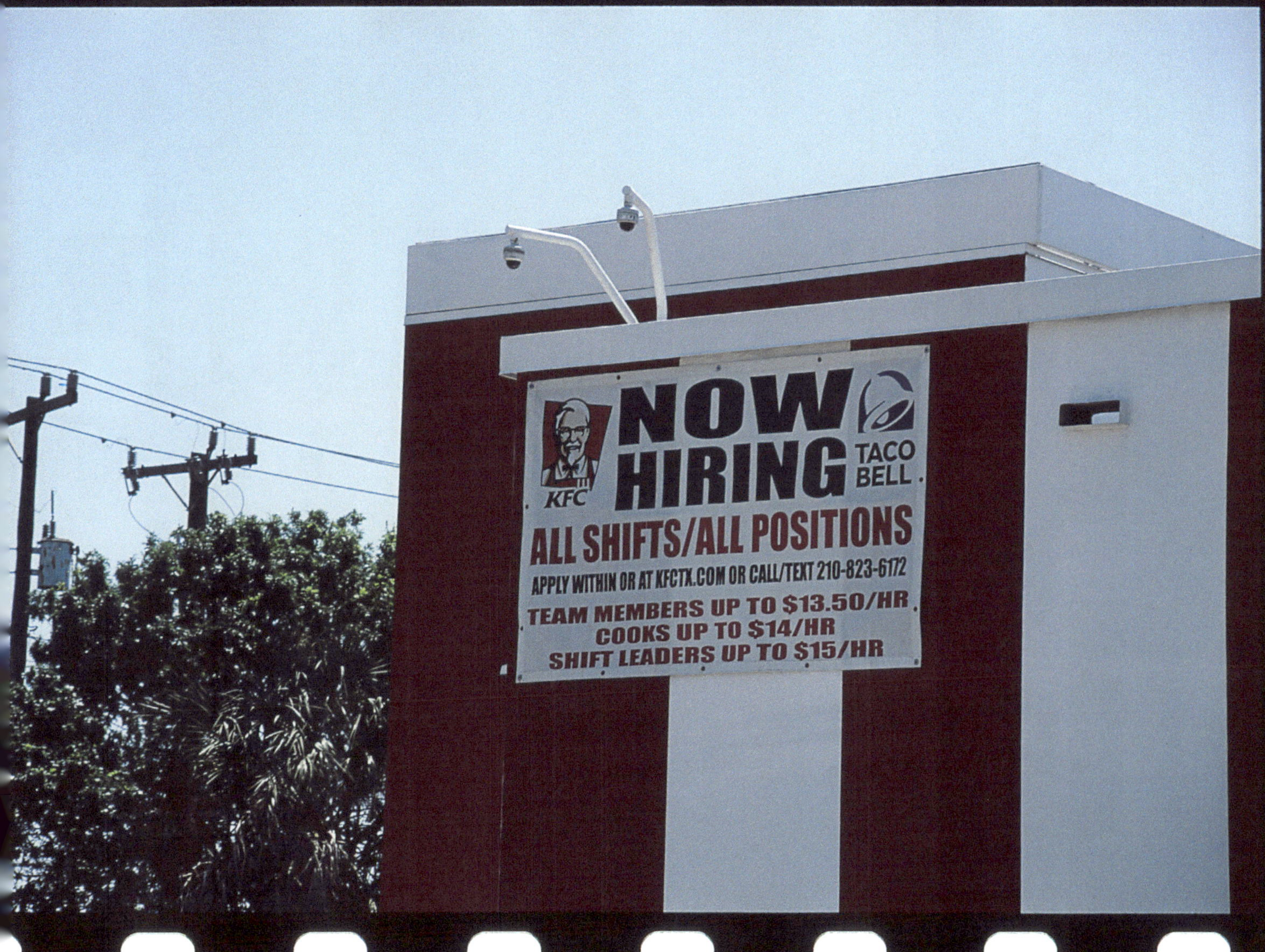
KFC
NOW
HIRING
TACO
BELL
ALL SHIFTS/ALL POSITIONS
APPLY WITHIN OR AT KFCTX.COM OR CALL/TEXT 210-823-6172
TEAM MEMBERS UP TO $13.50/HR
COOKS UP TO $14/HR
SHIFT LEADERS UP TO $15/HR

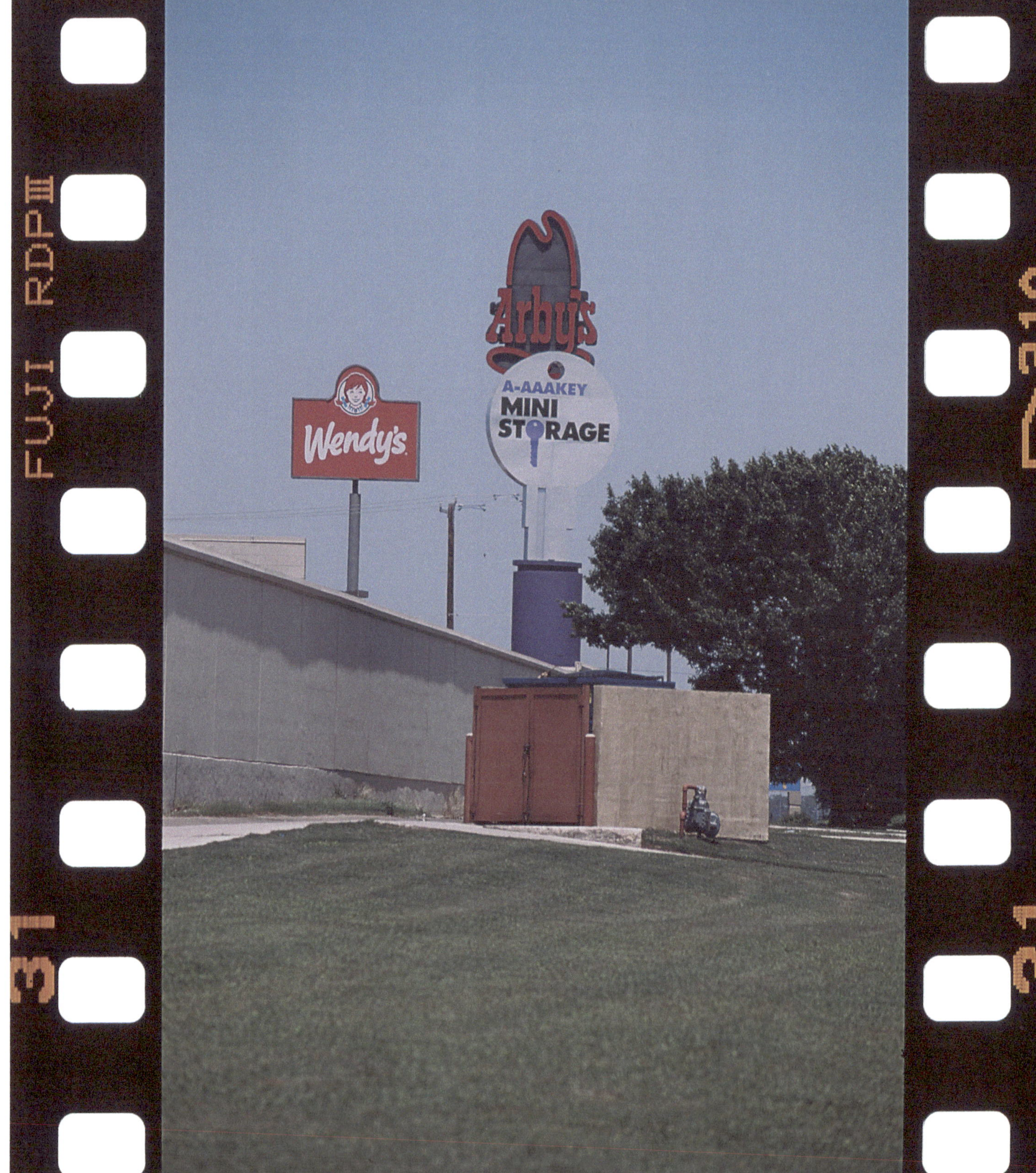
Arby's
A-AAAKEY
MINI
STORAGE
Wendy's
FUJI RDPⅢ
31
31

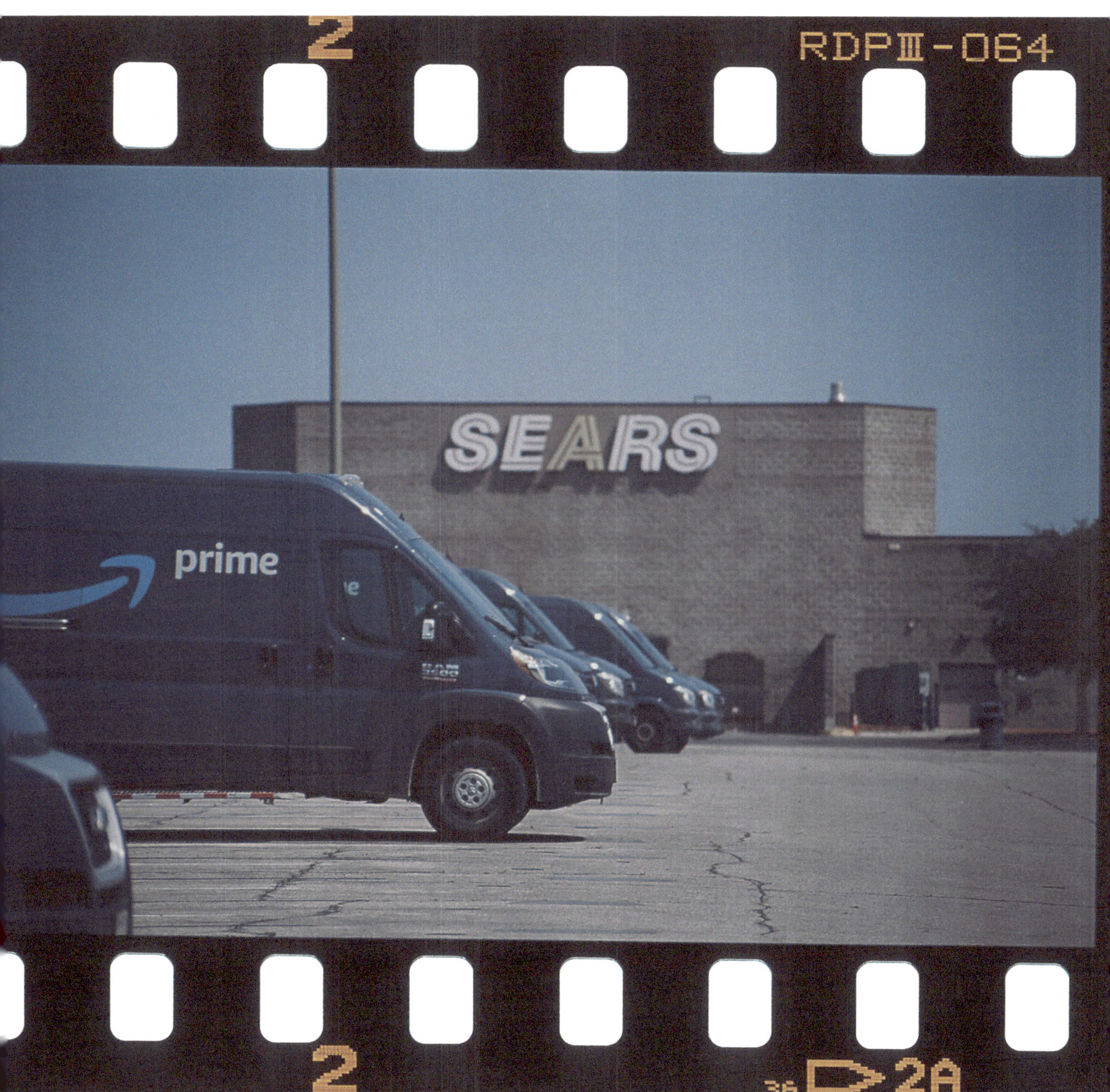

SEARS
prime

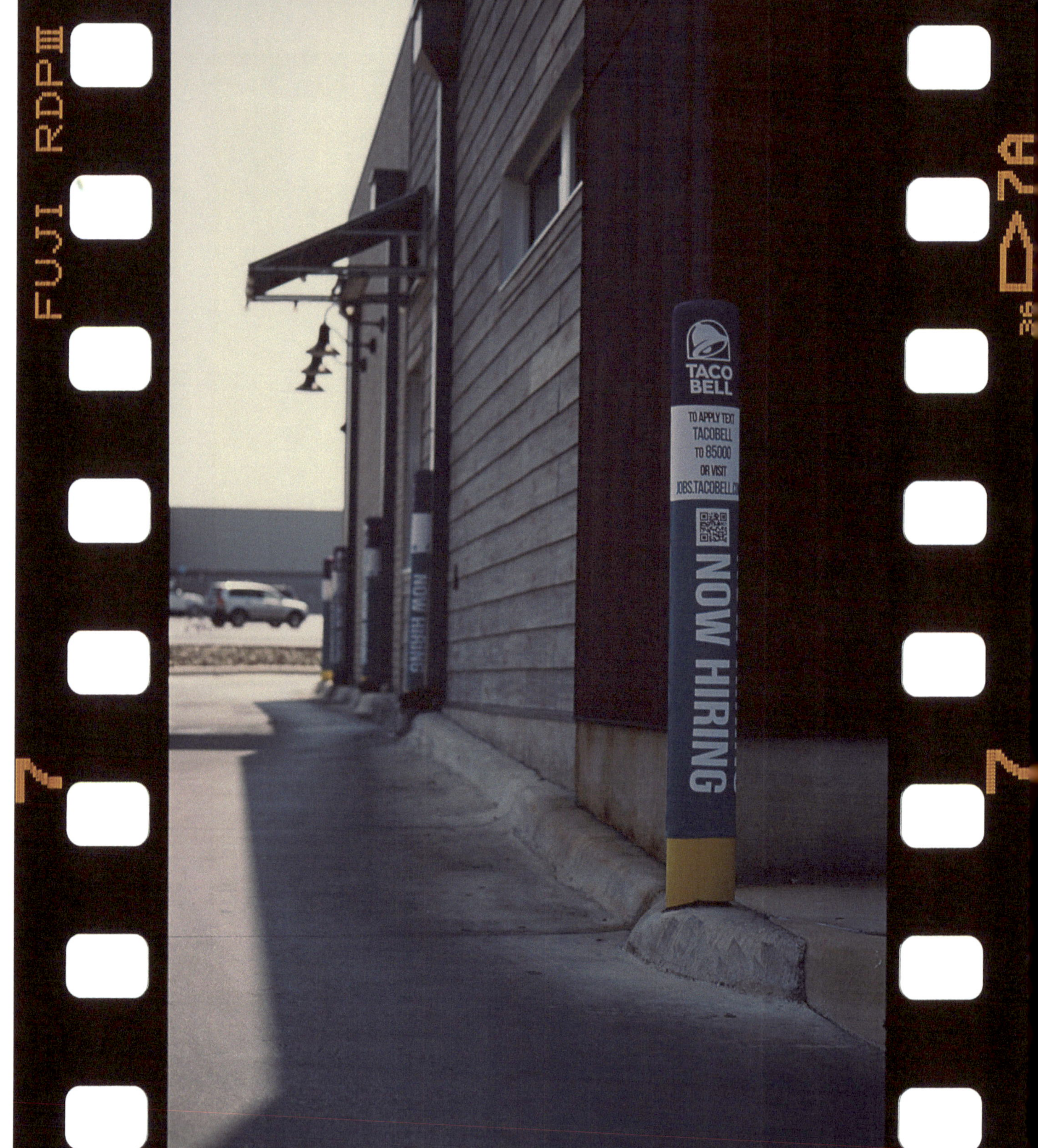
TACO
BELL
TO APPLY TEXT
TACOBELL
TO 85000
OR VISIT
JOBS.TACOBELL.COM
NOW HIRING

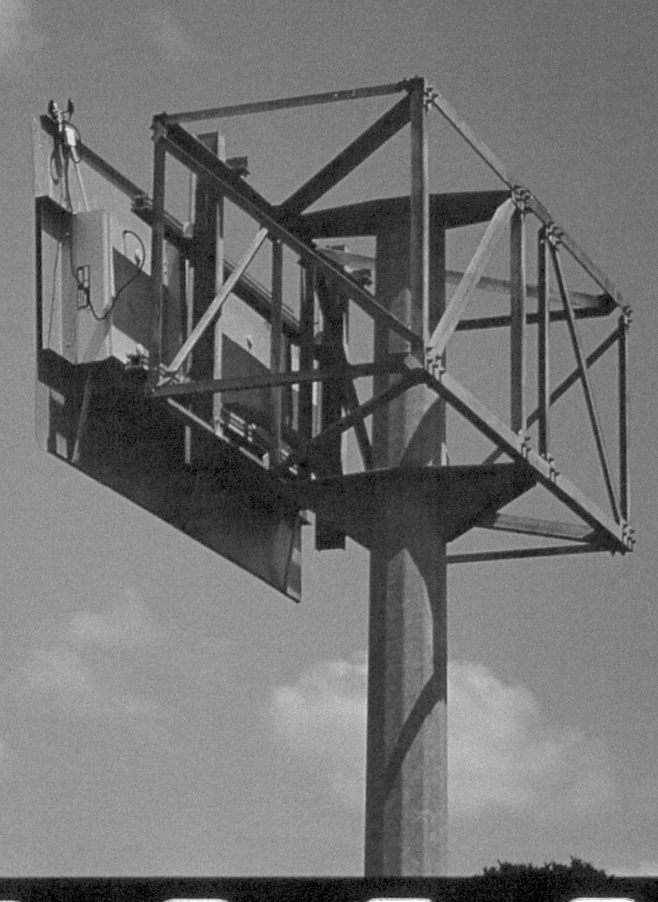

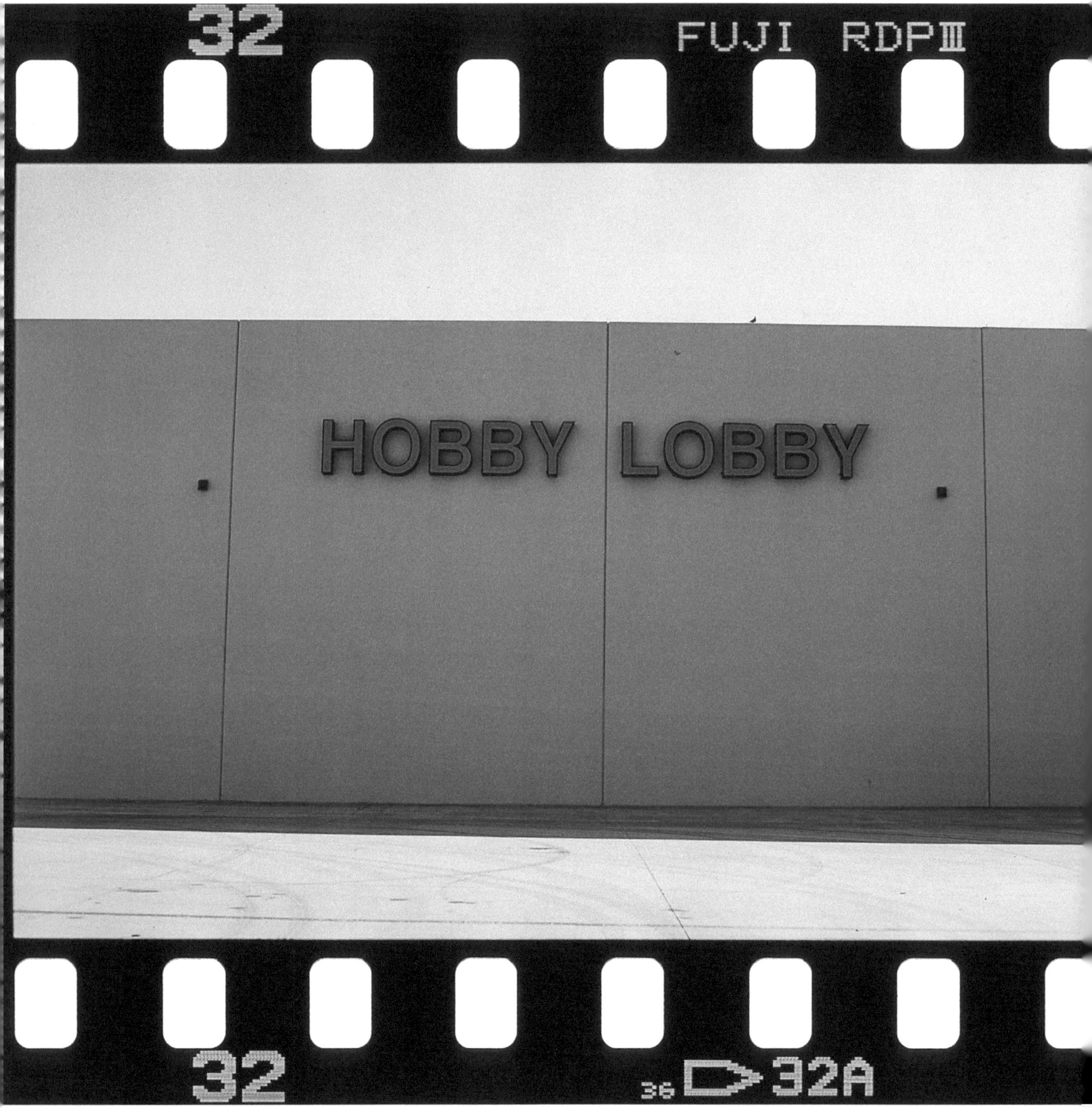

HOBBY LOBBY

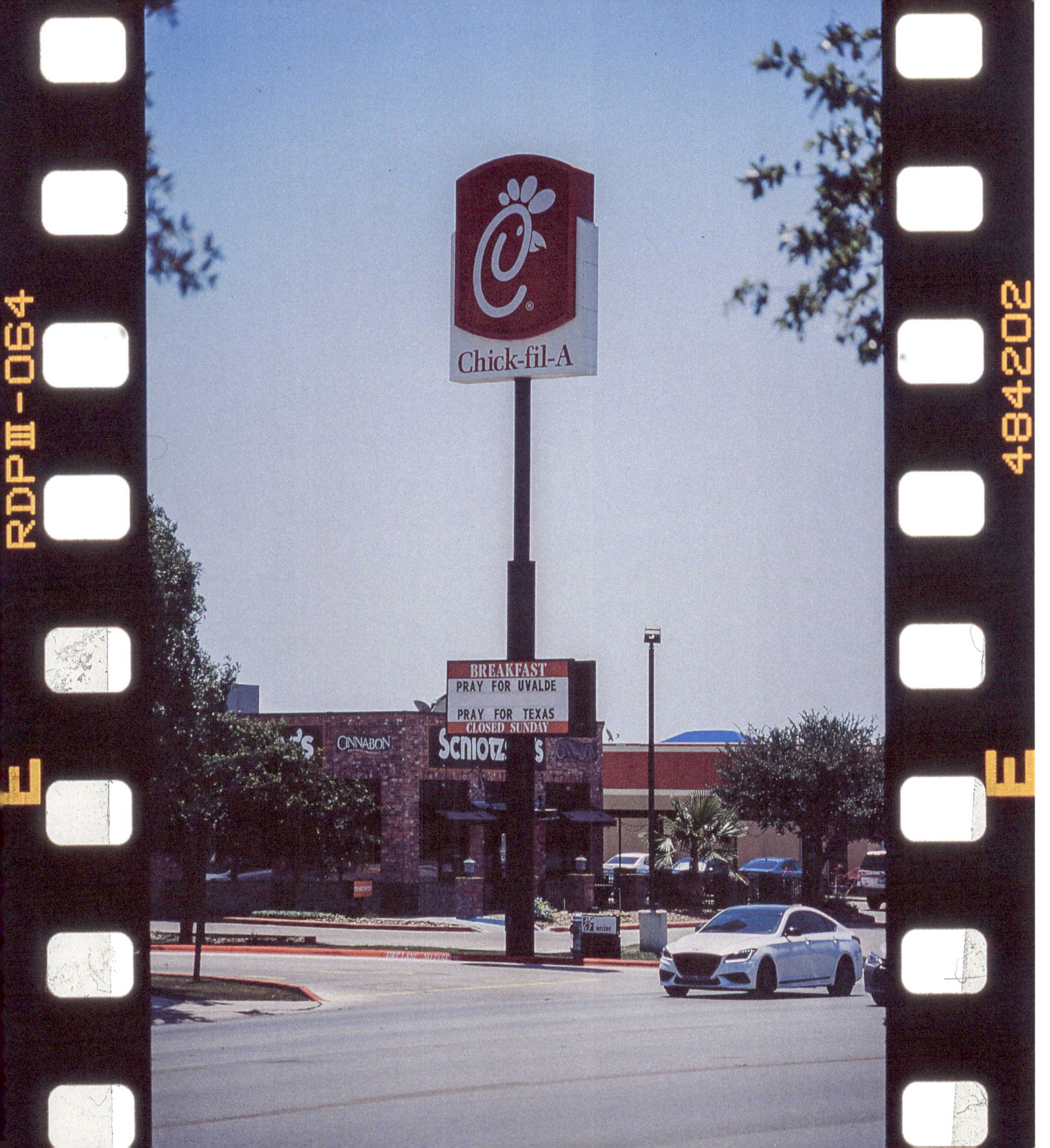

Chick-fil-A
BREAKFAST
PRAY FOR UVALDE
PRAY FOR TEXAS
CLOSED SUNDAY
CINNABON
Schlotzsky's
enter

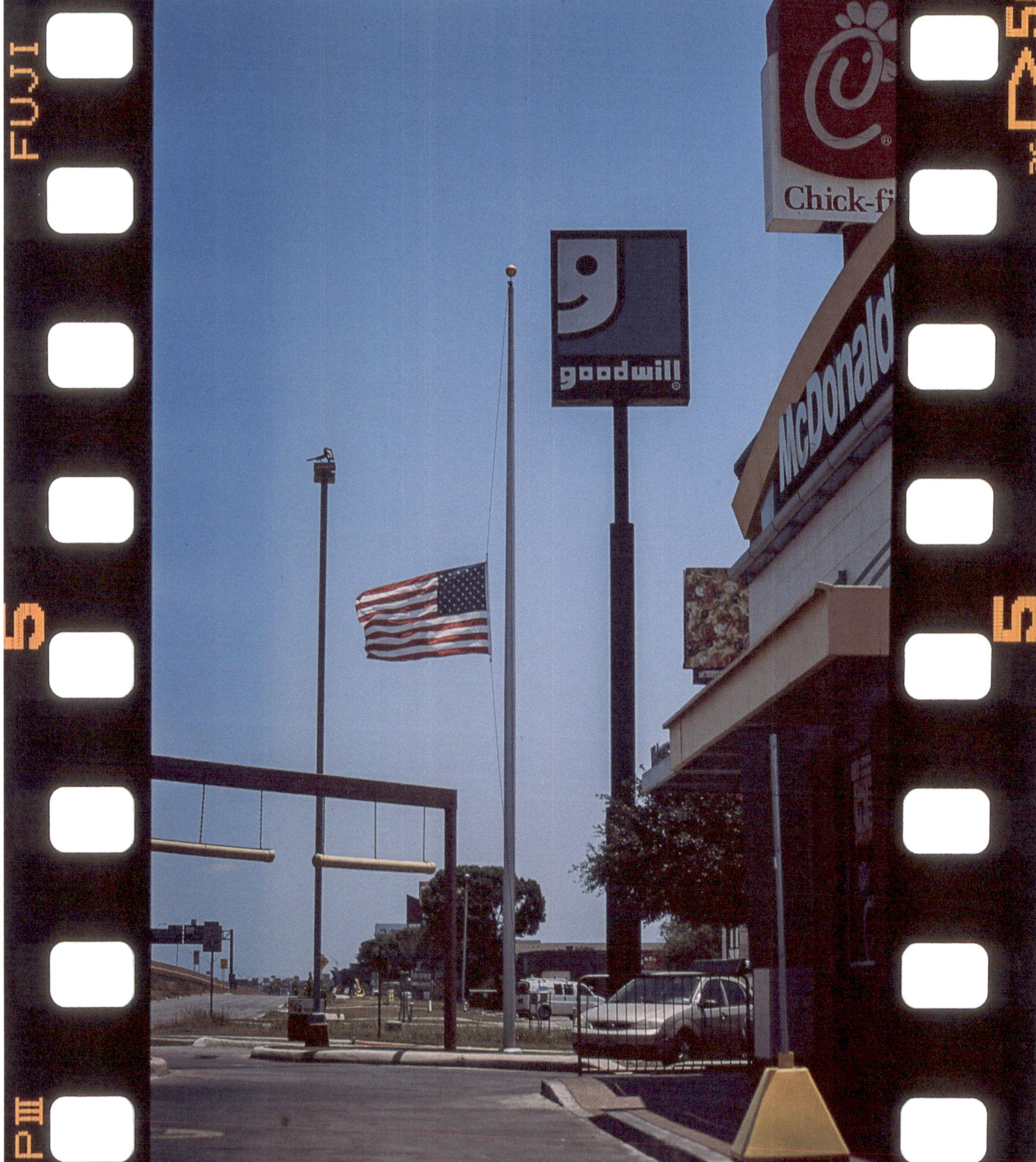
FUJI
Chick-fil-
goodwill
McDonald's

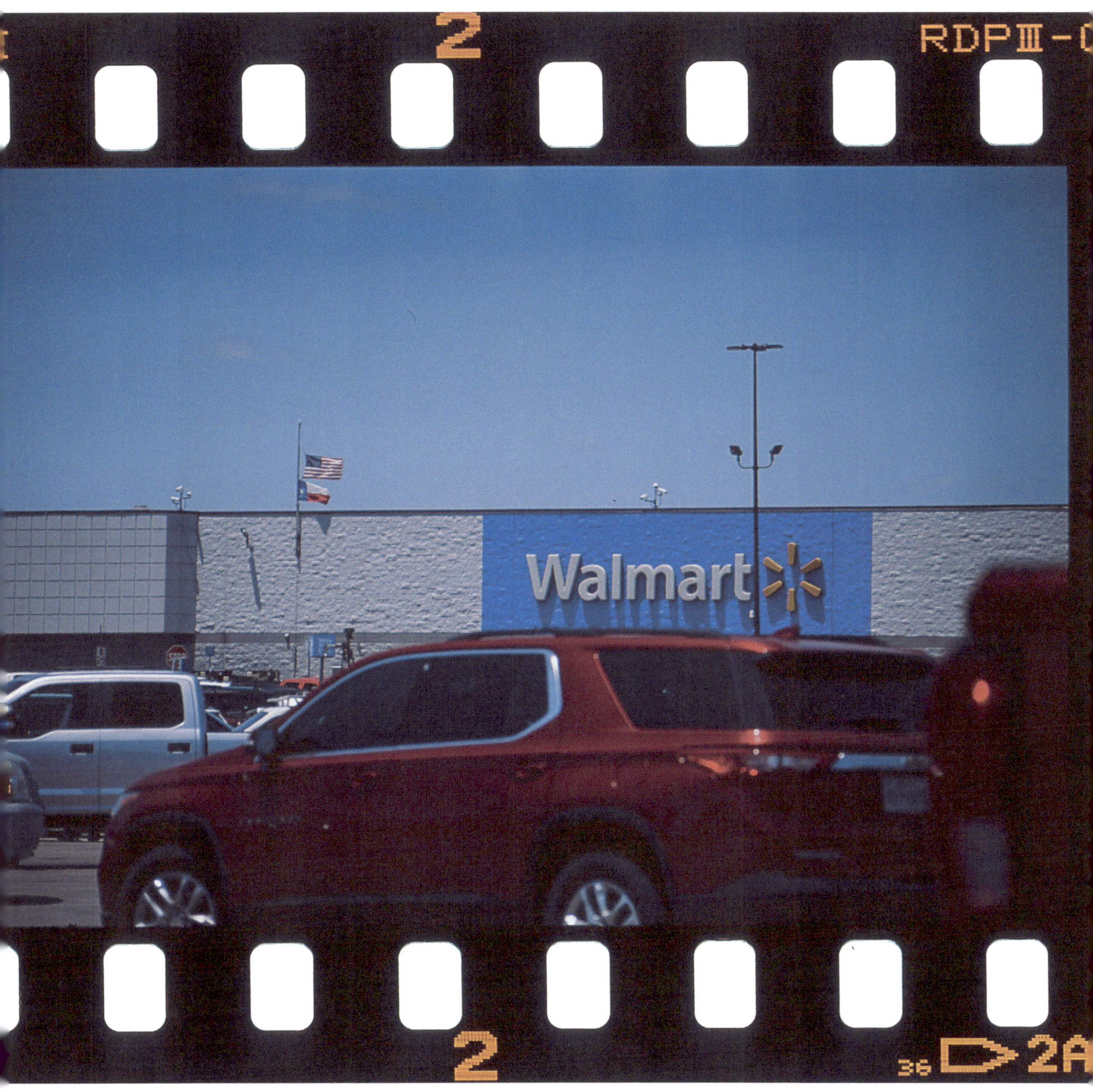
Walmart

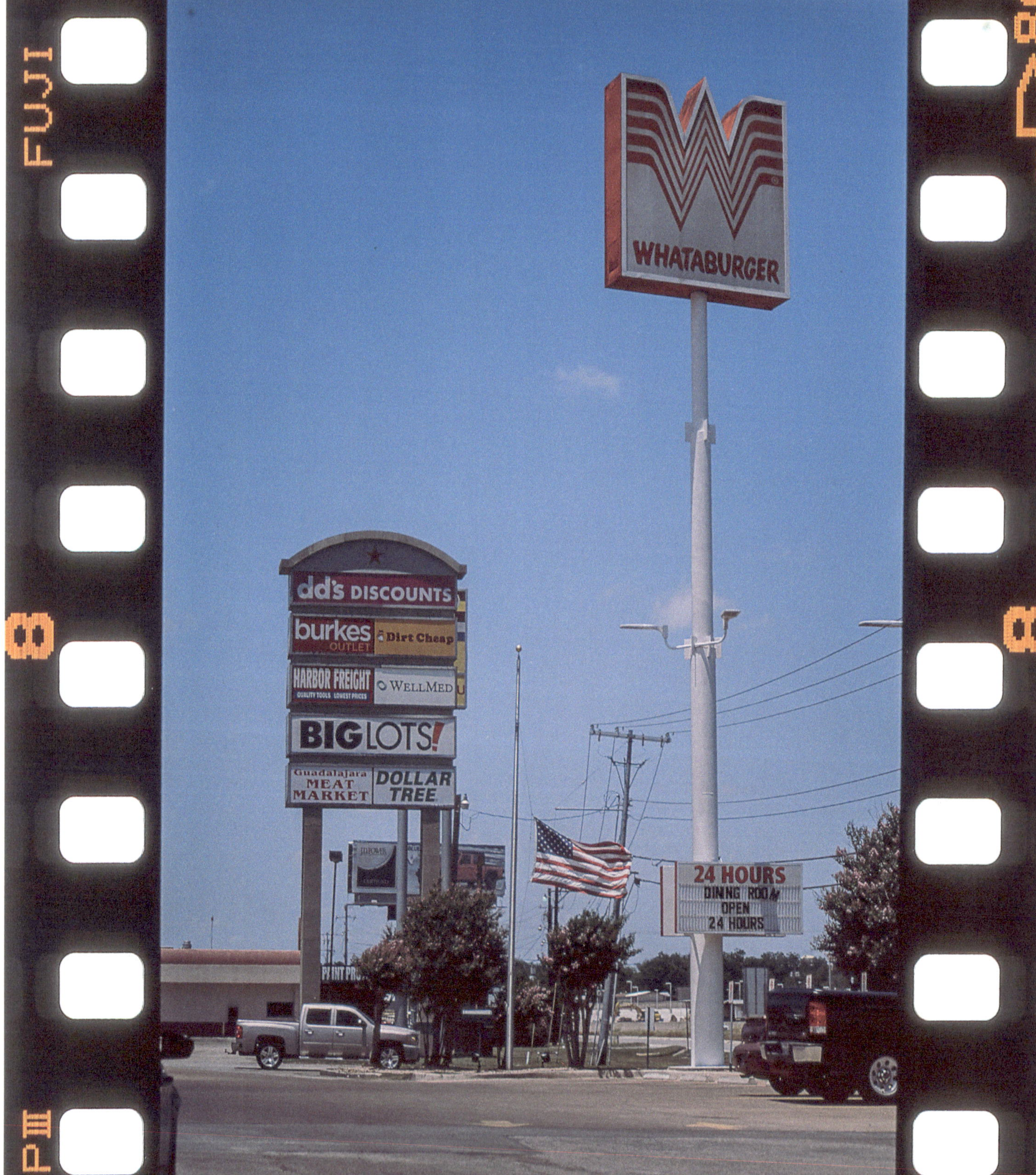

WHATABURGER
dd's DISCOUNTS
burkes OUTLET
Dirt Cheap
HARBOR FREIGHT
QUALITY TOOLS LOWEST PRICES
WellMed
BIG LOTS!
Guadalajara MEAT MARKET
DOLLAR TREE
24 HOURS
DINING ROOM
OPEN
24 HOURS
FUJI
8
P III

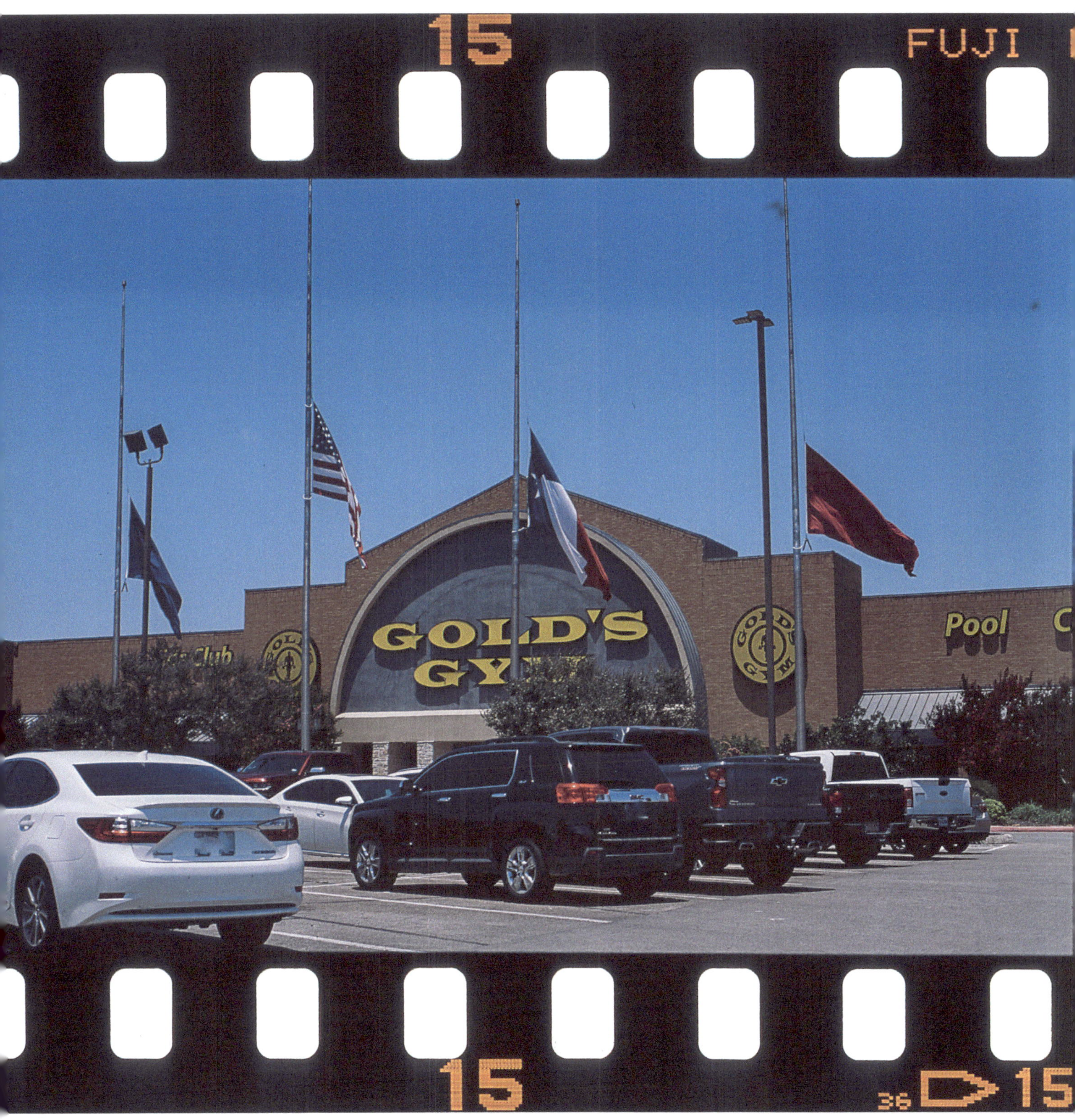

GOLD'S GYM
Pool
15
FUJI
15
36

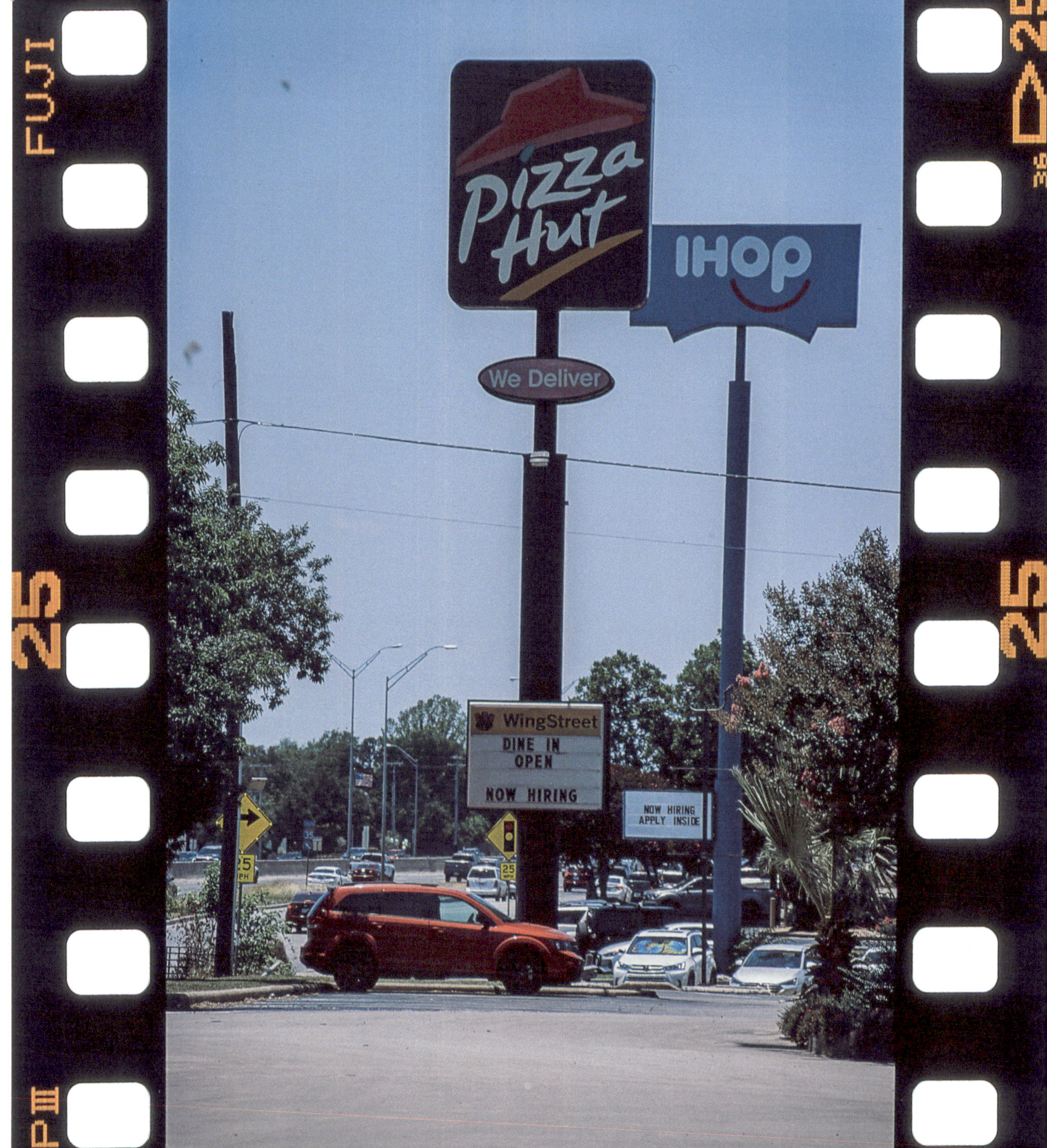
Pizza Hut
IHOP
We Deliver
WingStreet
DINE IN
OPEN
NOW HIRING
NOW HIRING
APPLY INSIDE
25
MPH
25
MPH

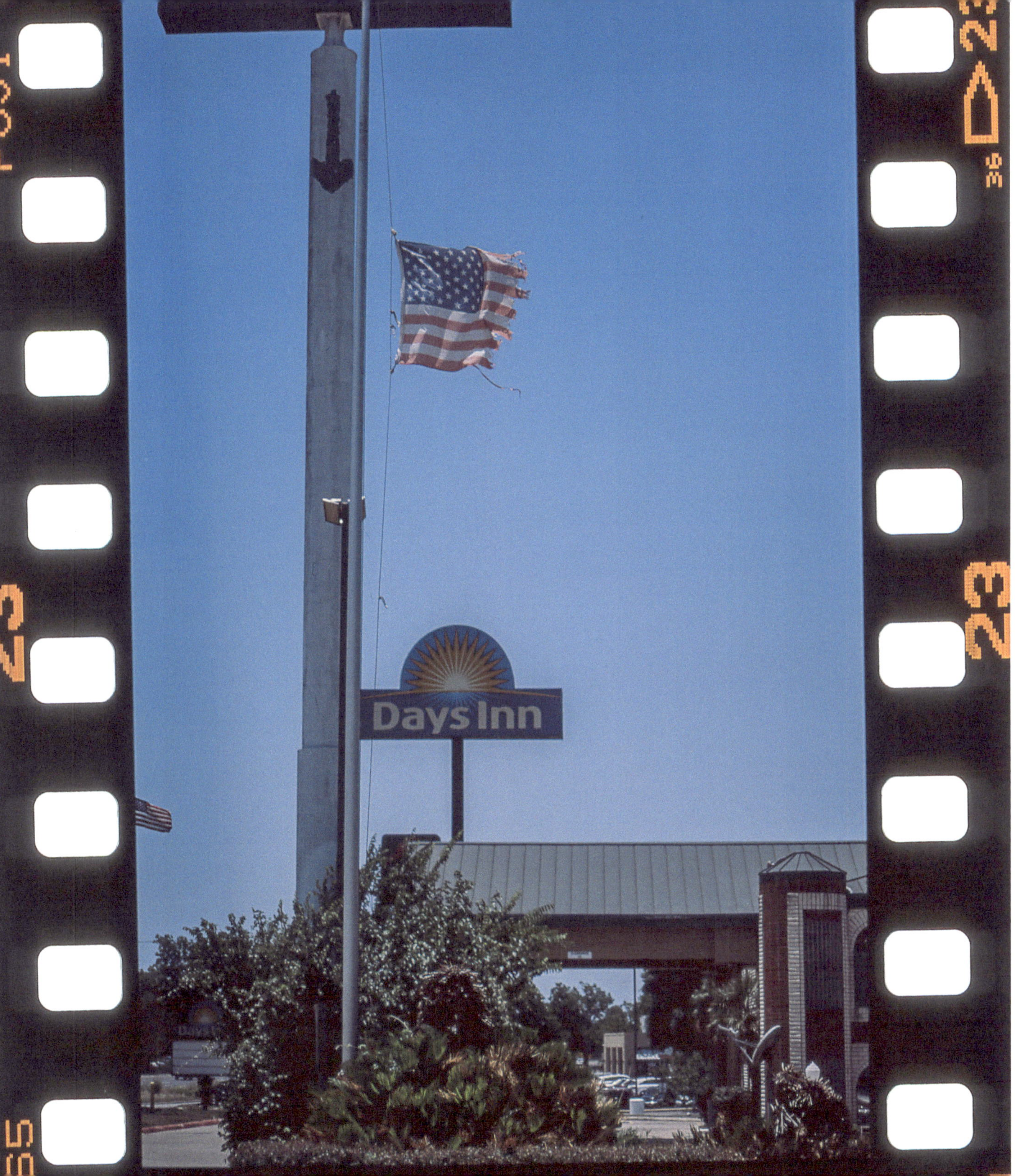
Days Inn

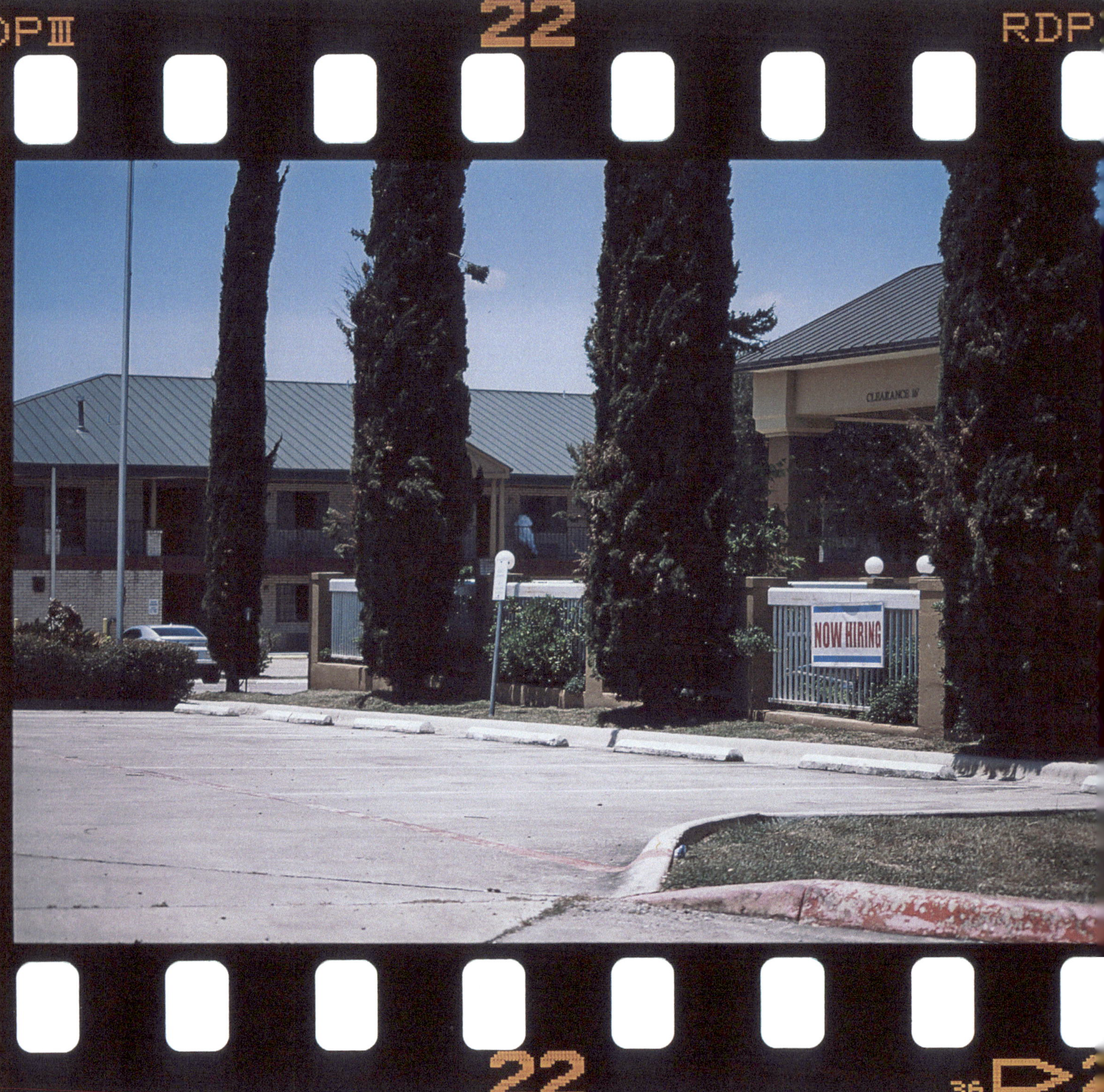

CLEARANCE 10'
NOW HIRING

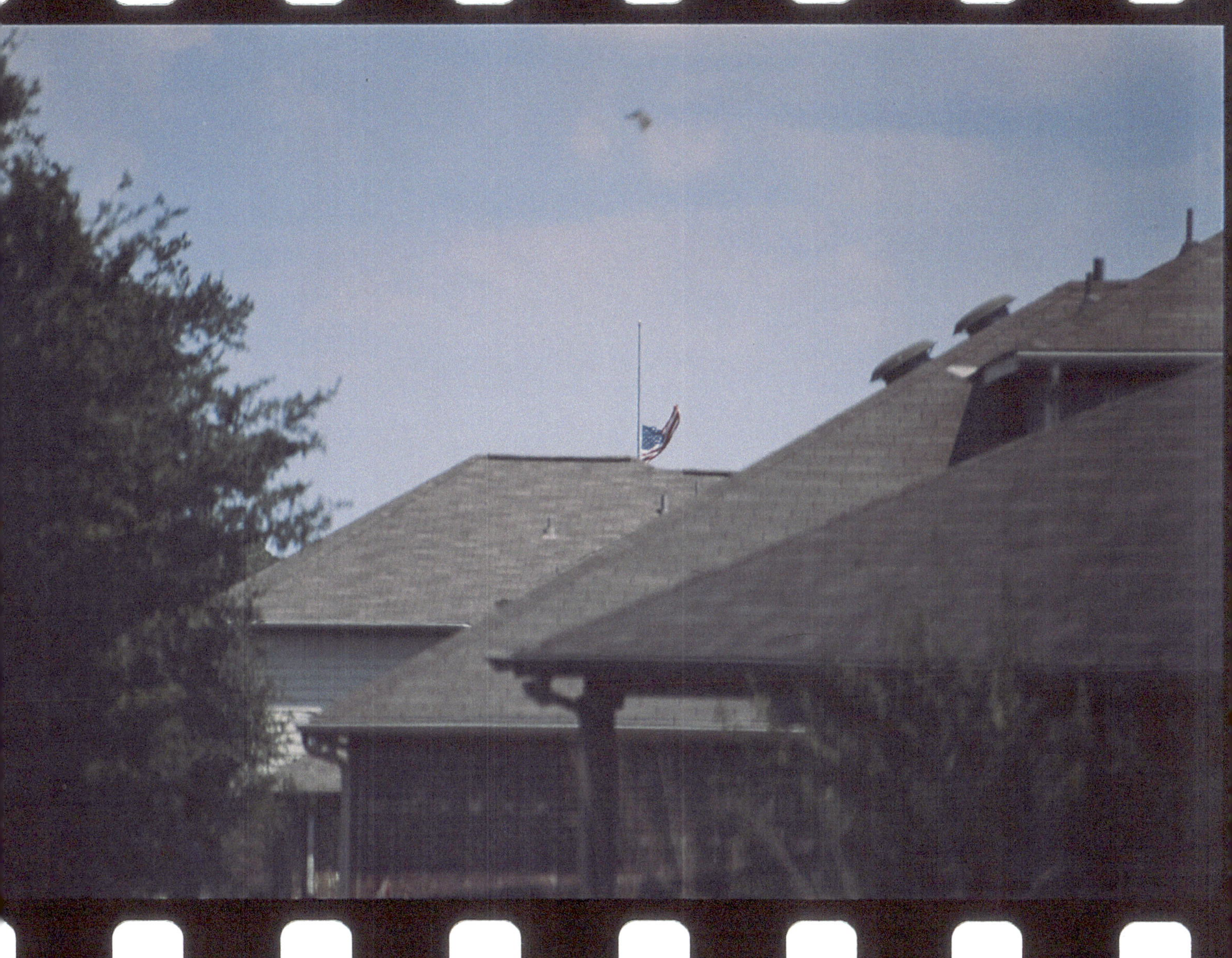
15
FUJI RDPⅢ
15
36 ▷ 15A

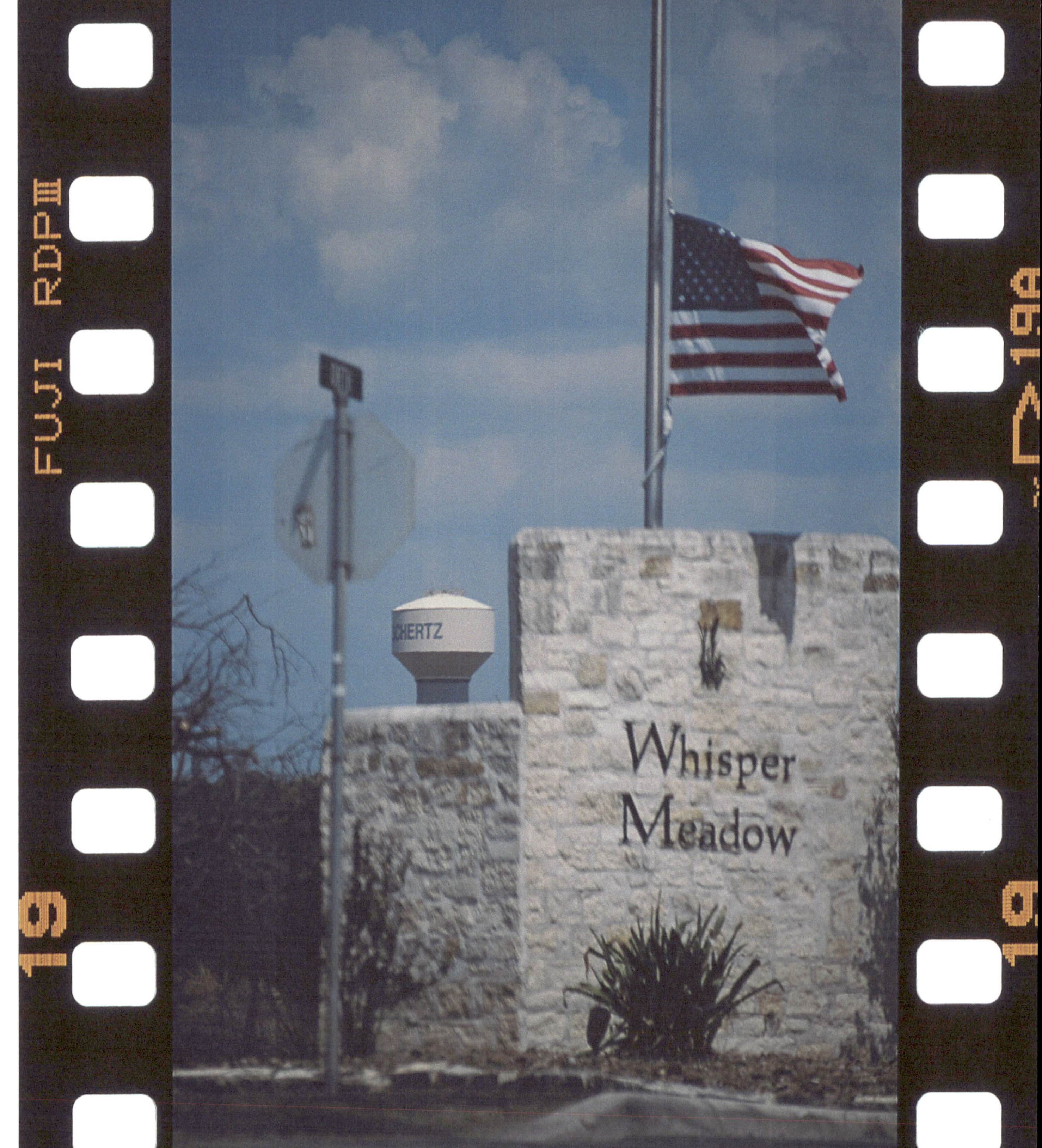
SCHERTZ
Whisper
Meadow

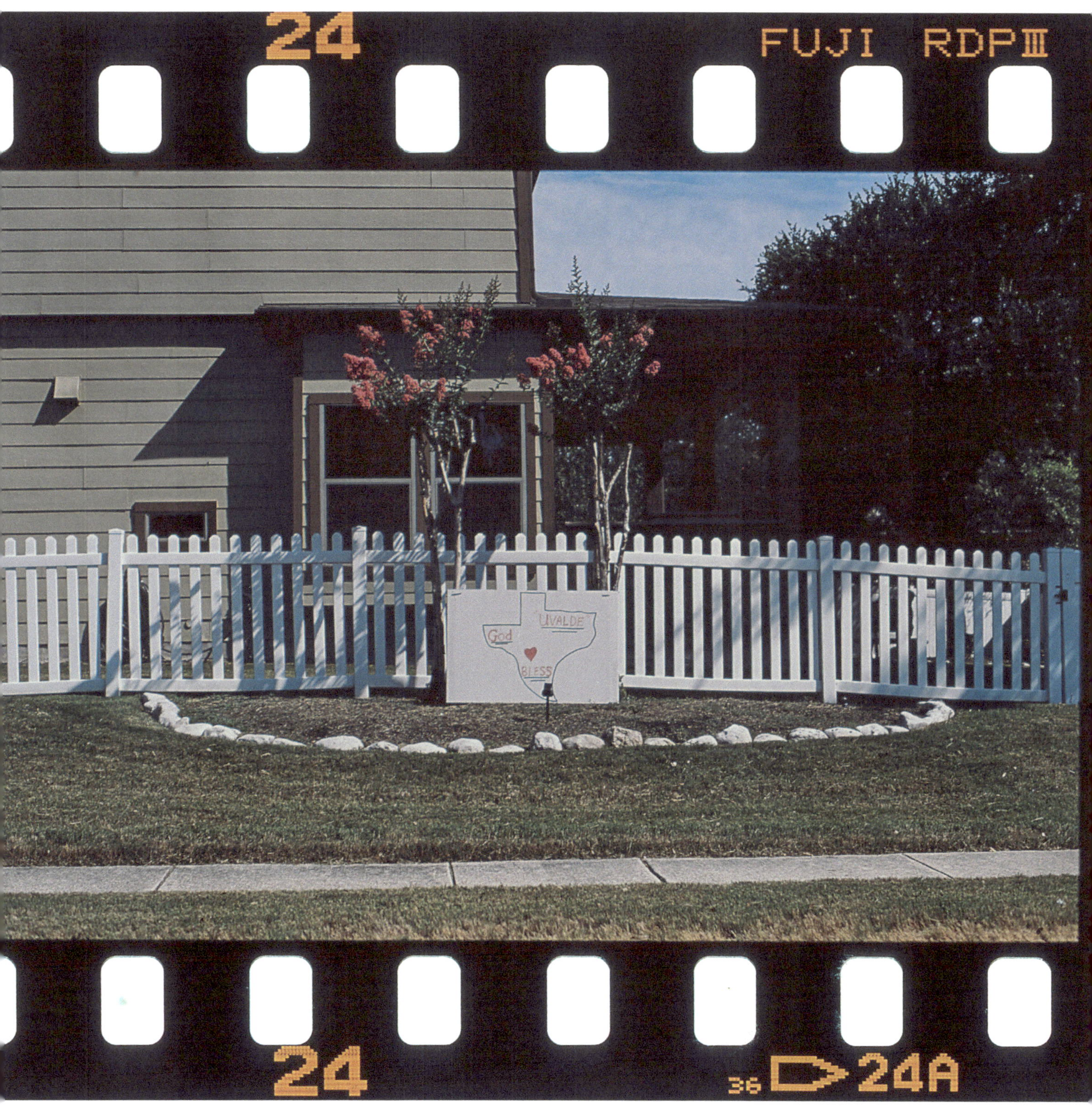
God
UVALDE
BLESS

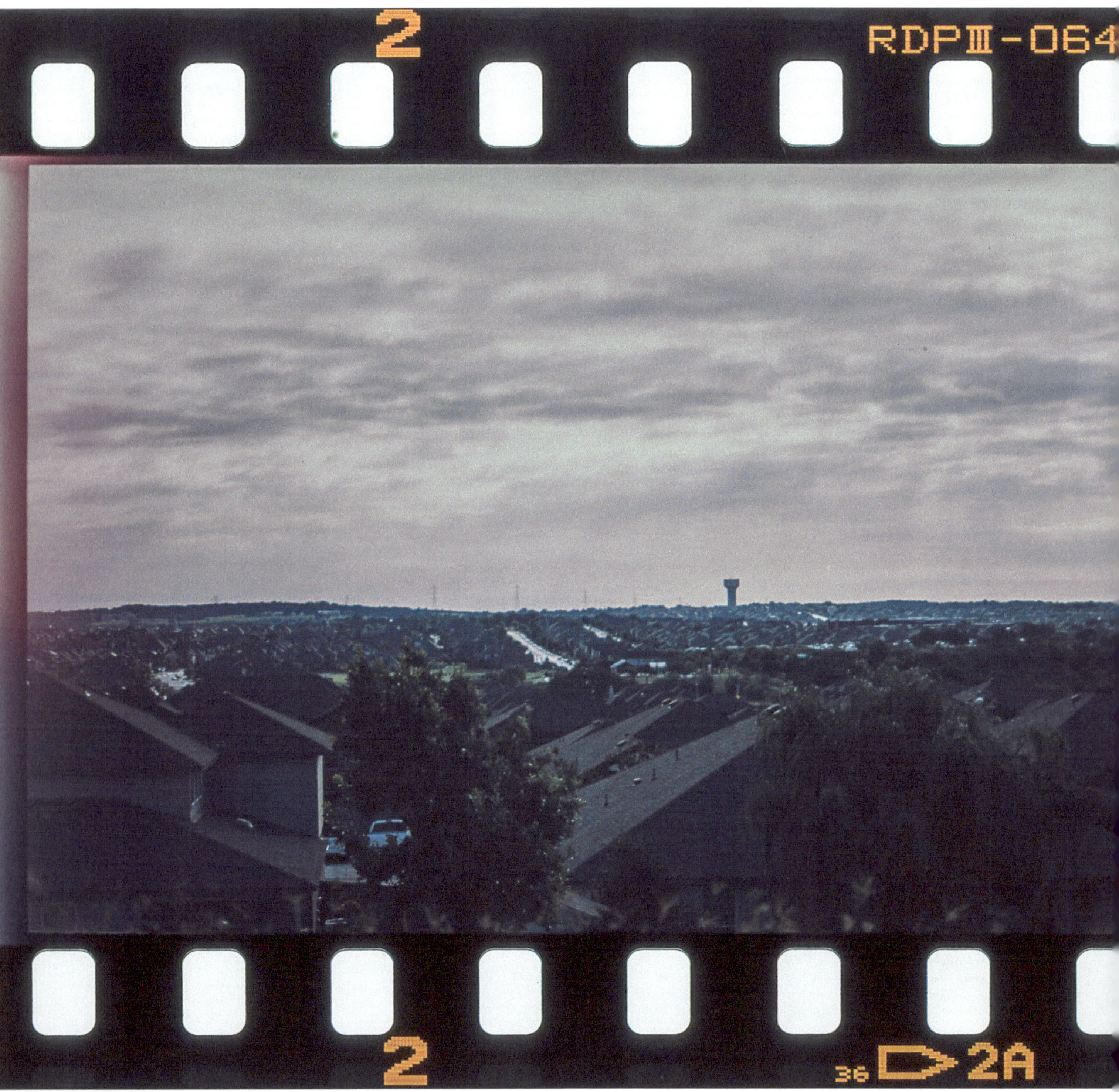
2
RDPⅢ-064
36
2A
2

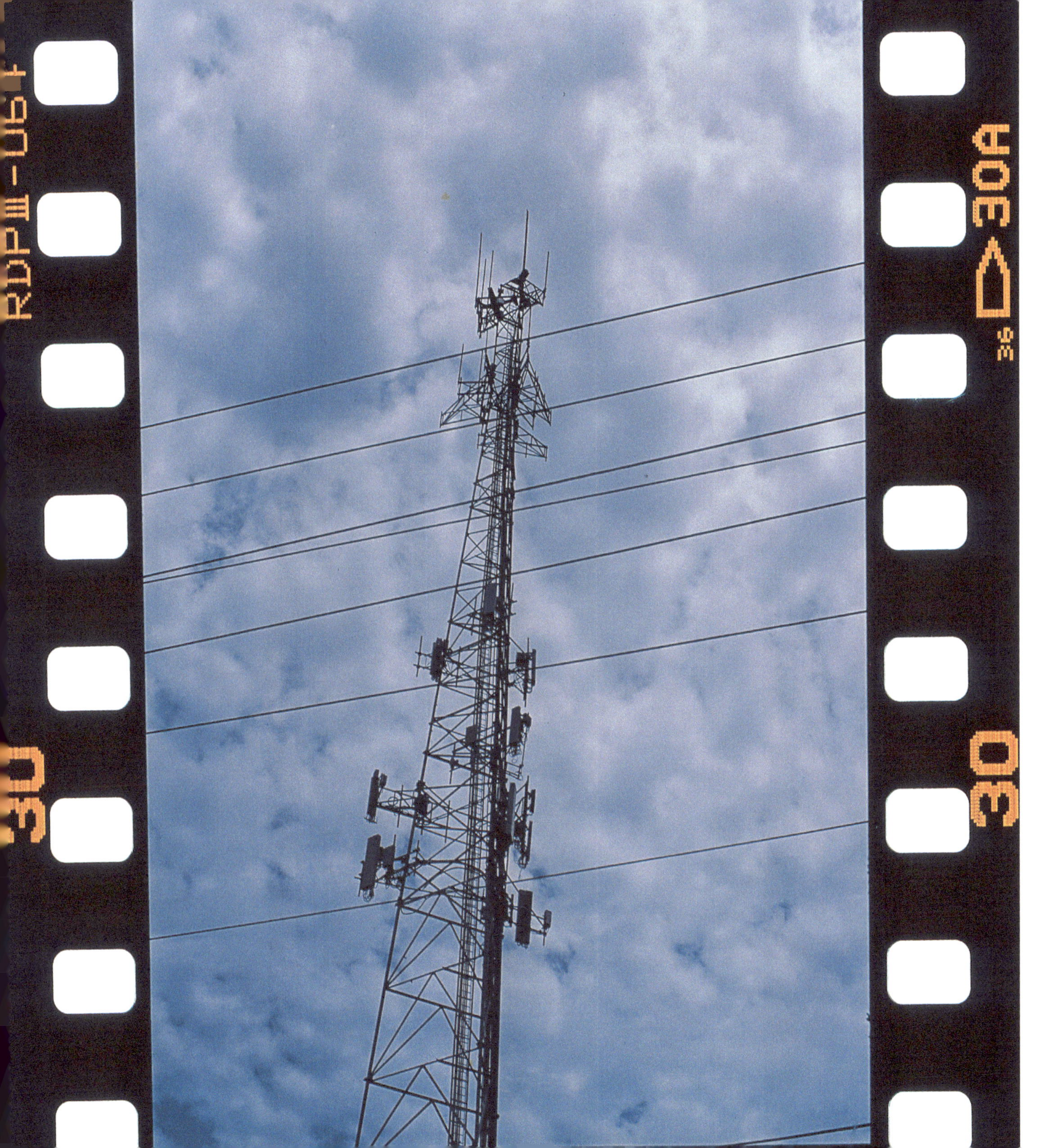

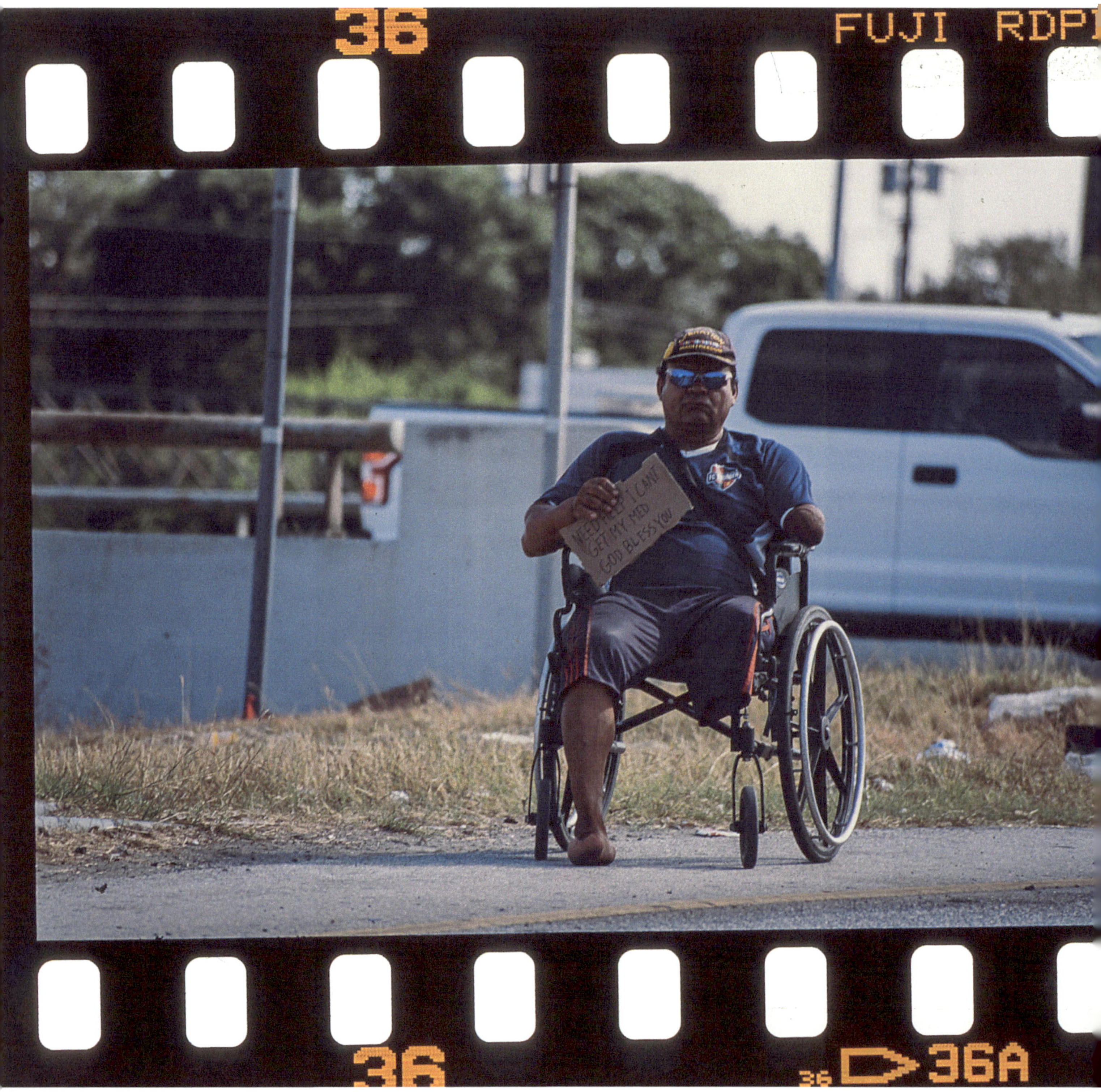
NEED HELP I CANT
GET MY MED
GOD BLESS YOU

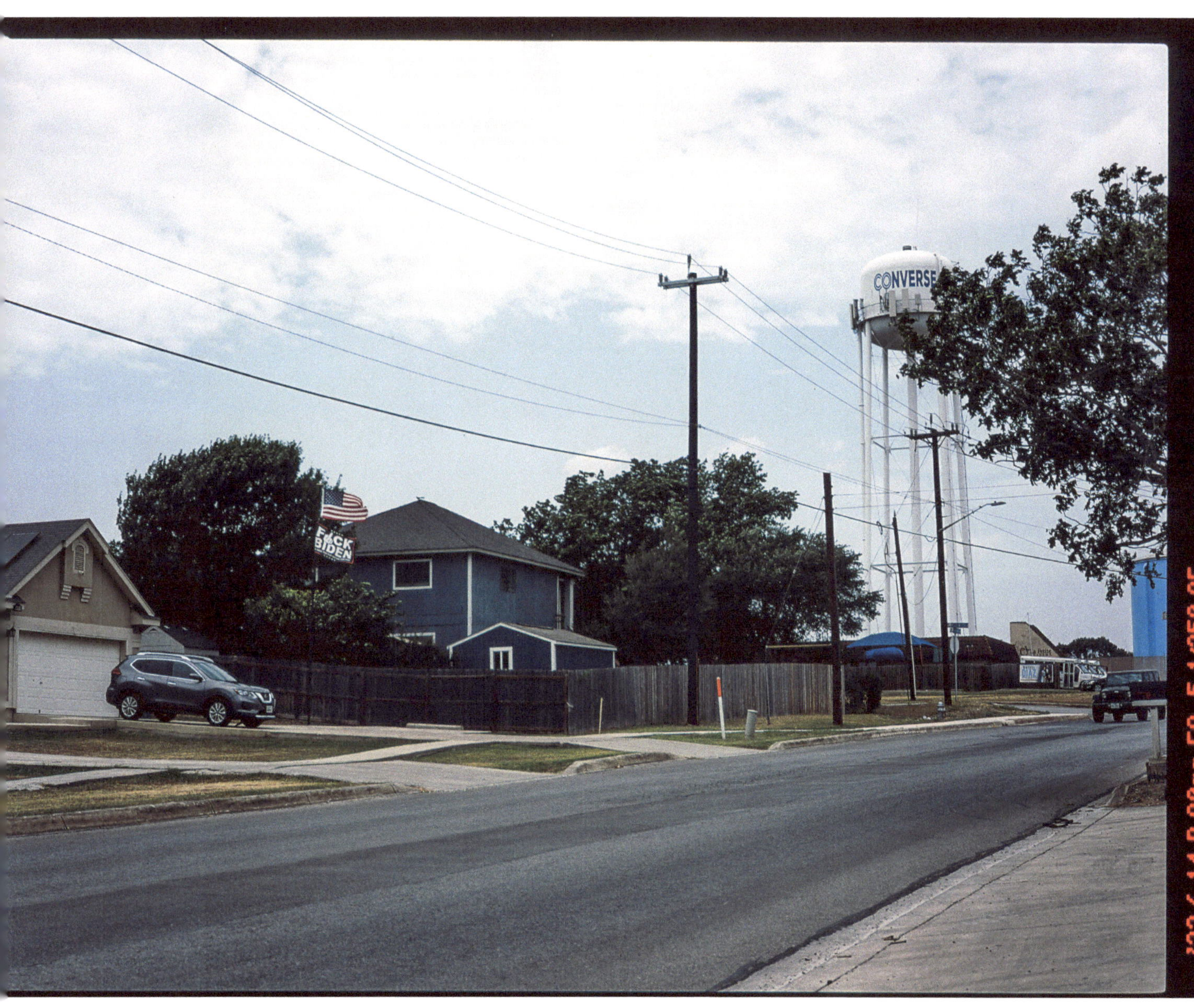

CONVERSE
F*CK BIDEN
'22 6 14 P 90mm F9.5 1/250 AF

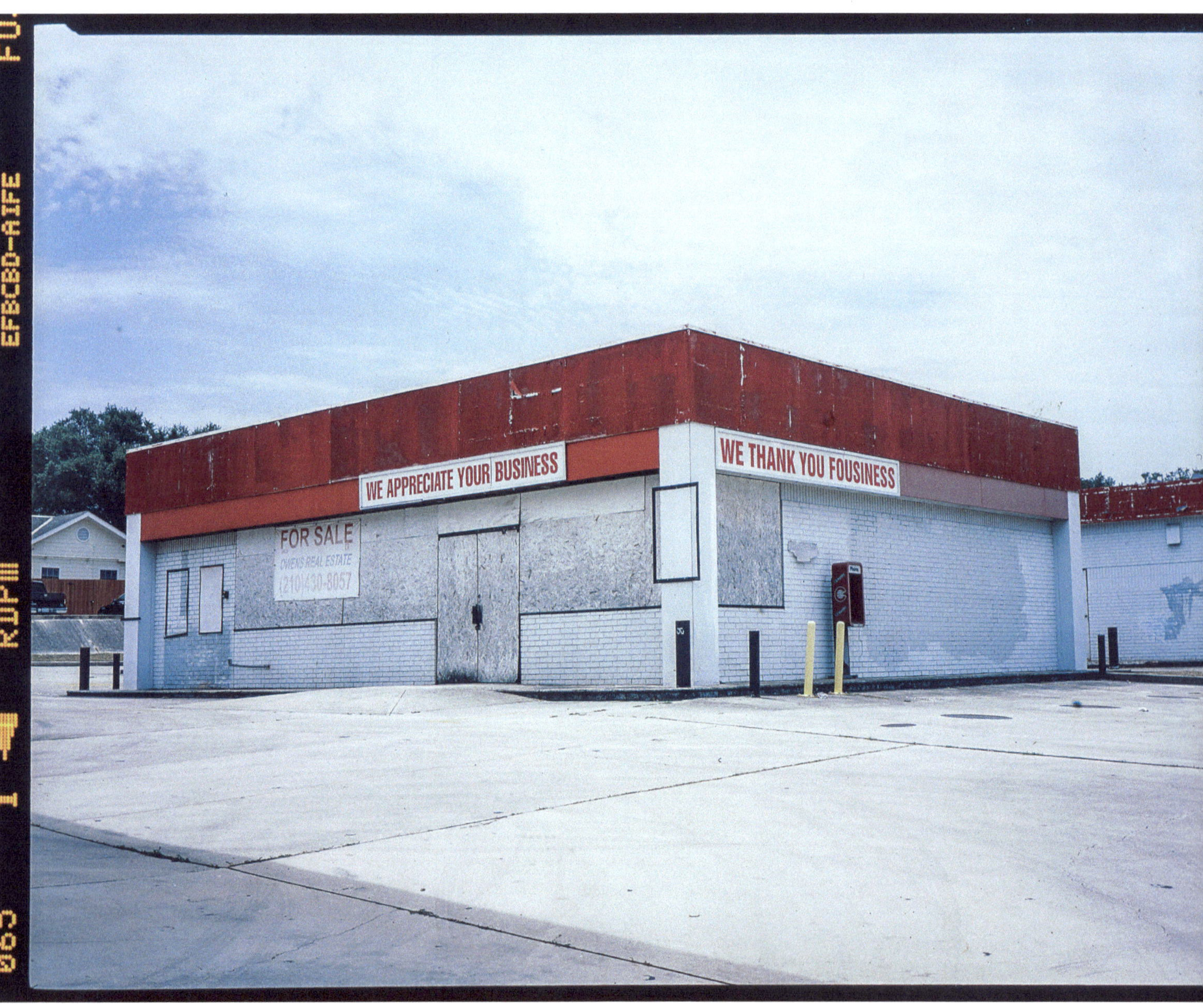

WE APPRECIATE YOUR BUSINESS
WE THANK YOU FOUSINESS
FOR SALE
OWENS REAL ESTATE
(210) 430-8057

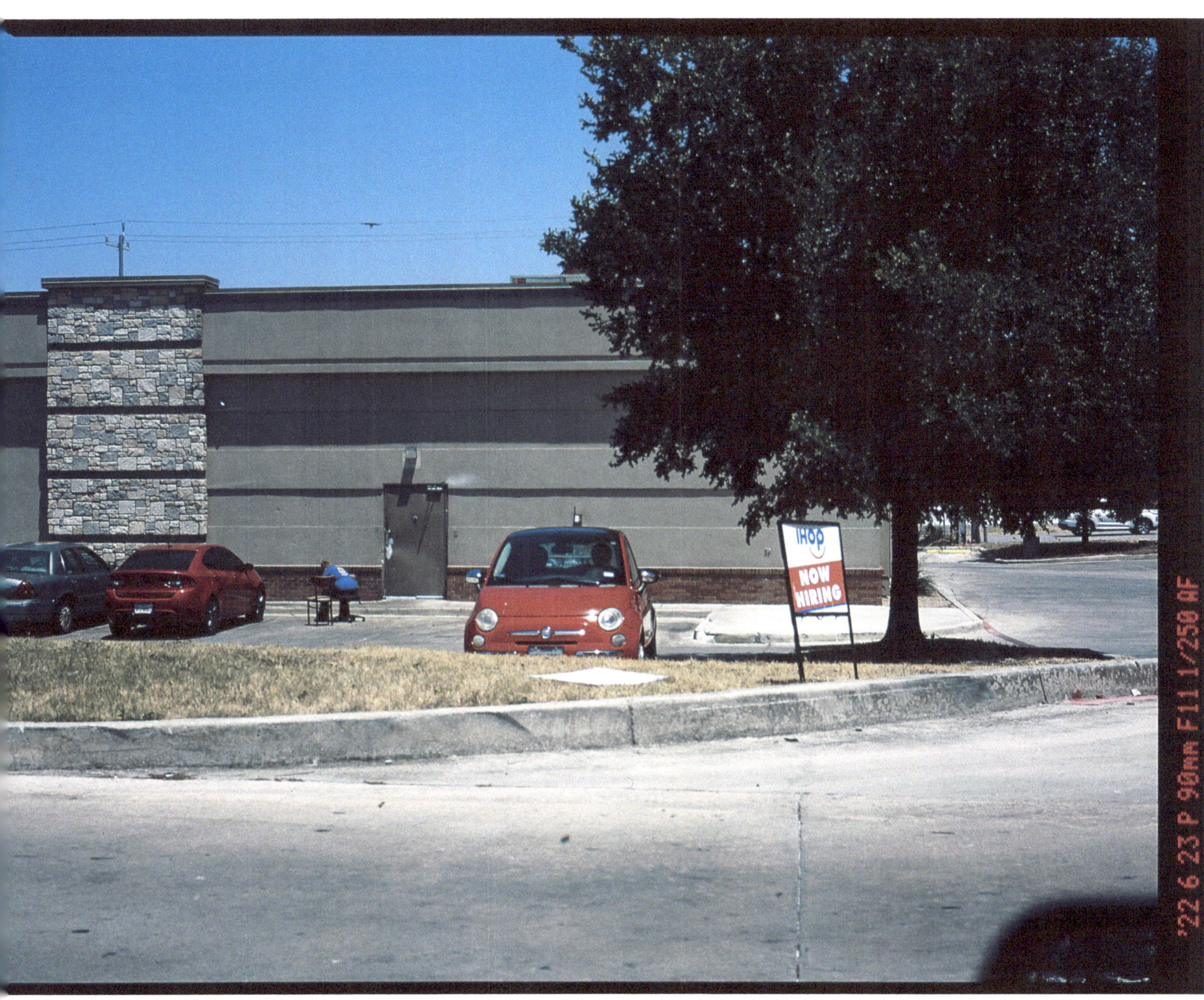

IHOP
NOW
HIRING

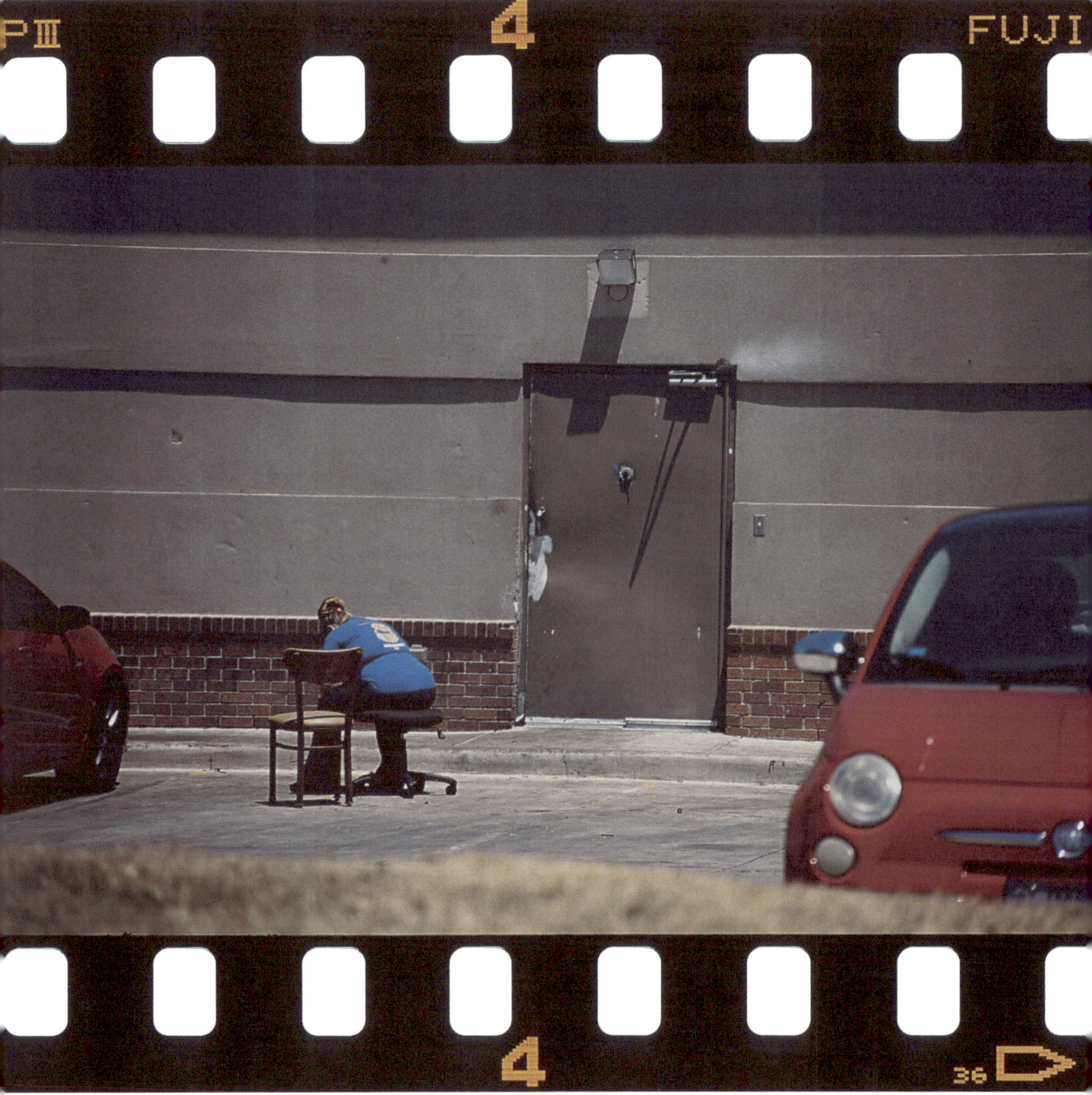

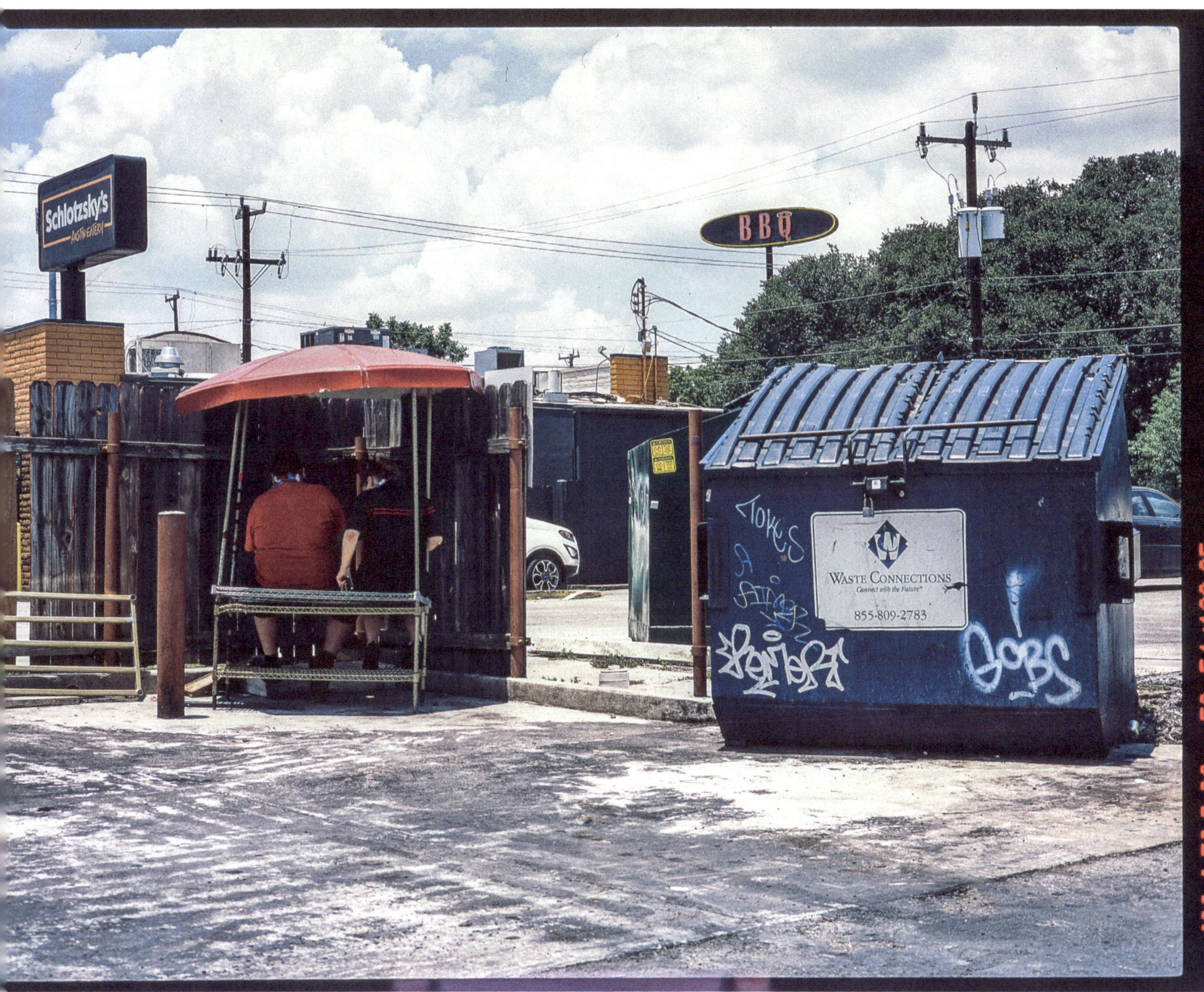

Schlotzsky's
AUSTIN EATERY
BBQ
WASTE CONNECTIONS
Connect with the Future®
855-809-2783

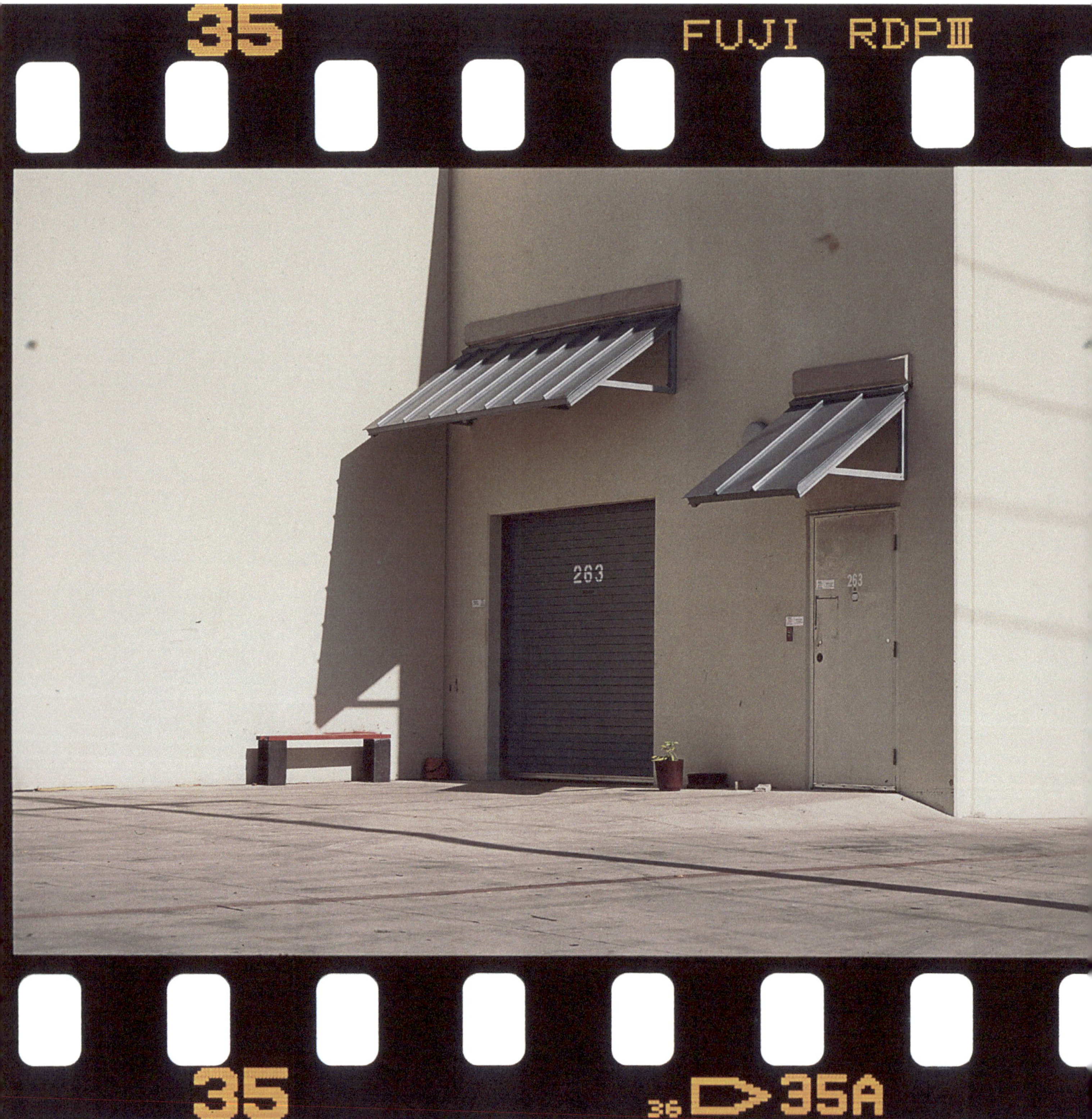
35
FUJI RDPIII
263
263
35
36 35A

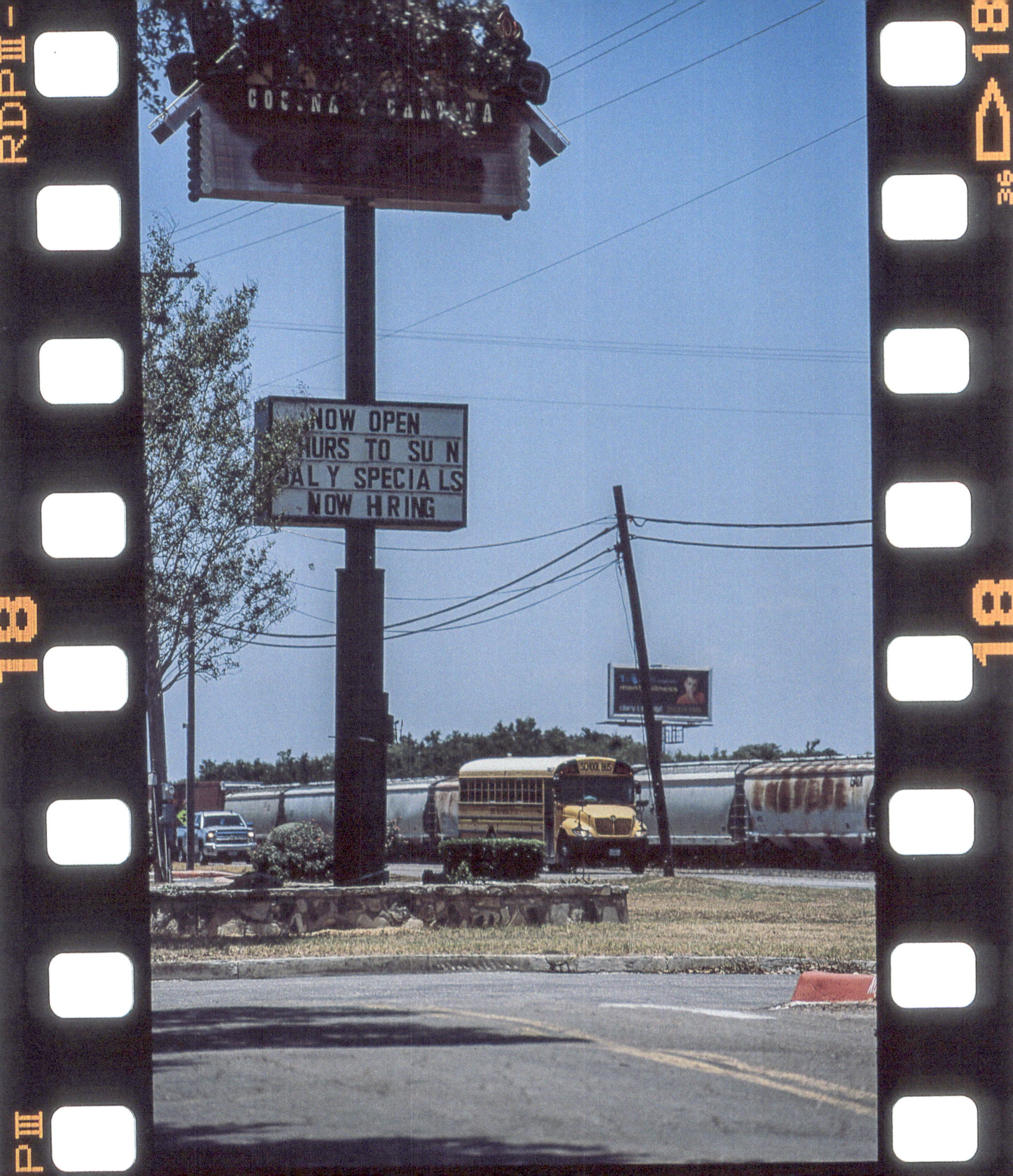
COCINA Y CANTINA
NOW OPEN
THURS TO SUN
DAILY SPECIALS
NOW HRING
SCHOOL BUS

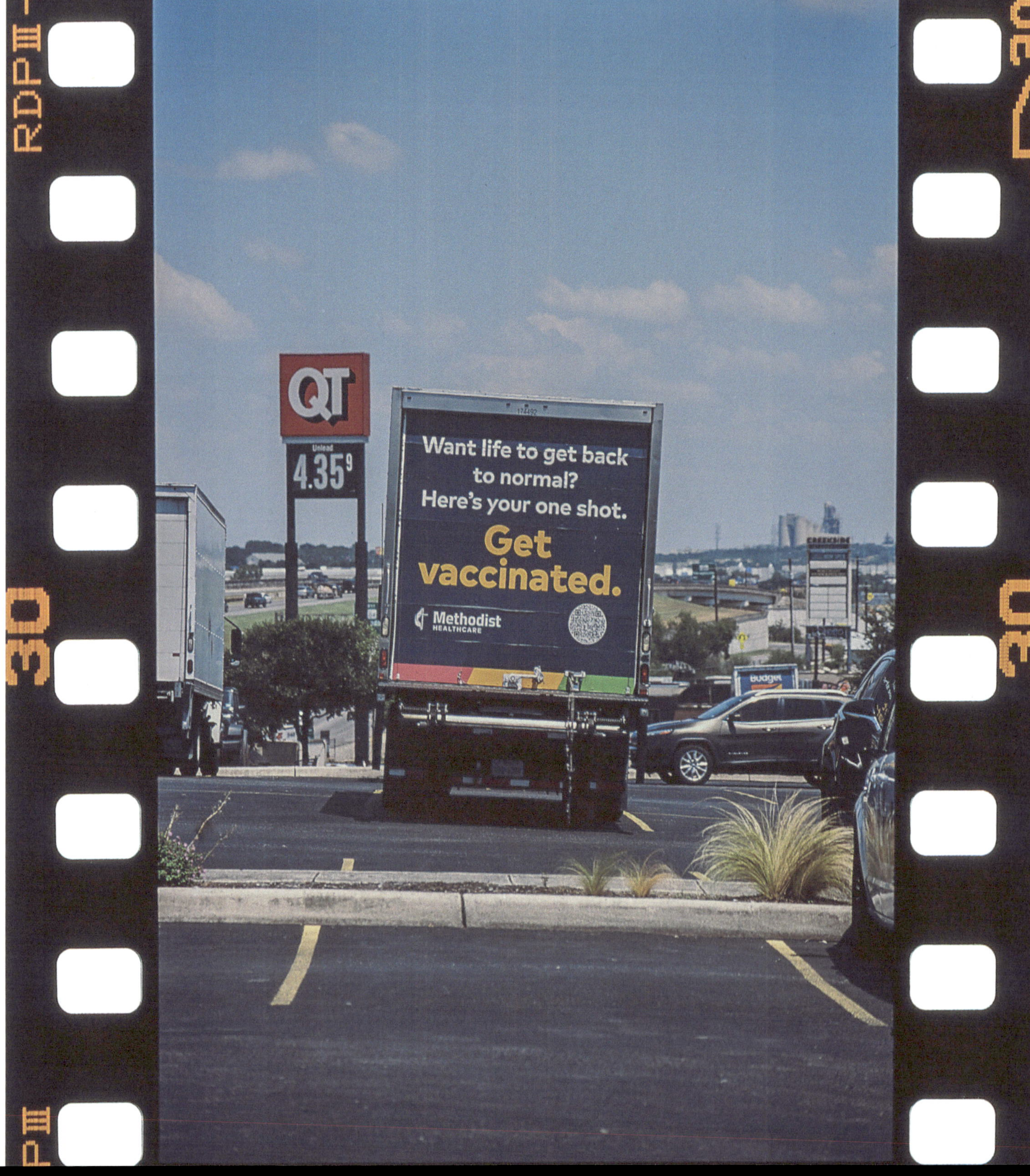
QT
Unlead
4.35 9
Want life to get back
to normal?
Here's your one shot.
Get
vaccinated.
Methodist
HEALTHCARE
Budget

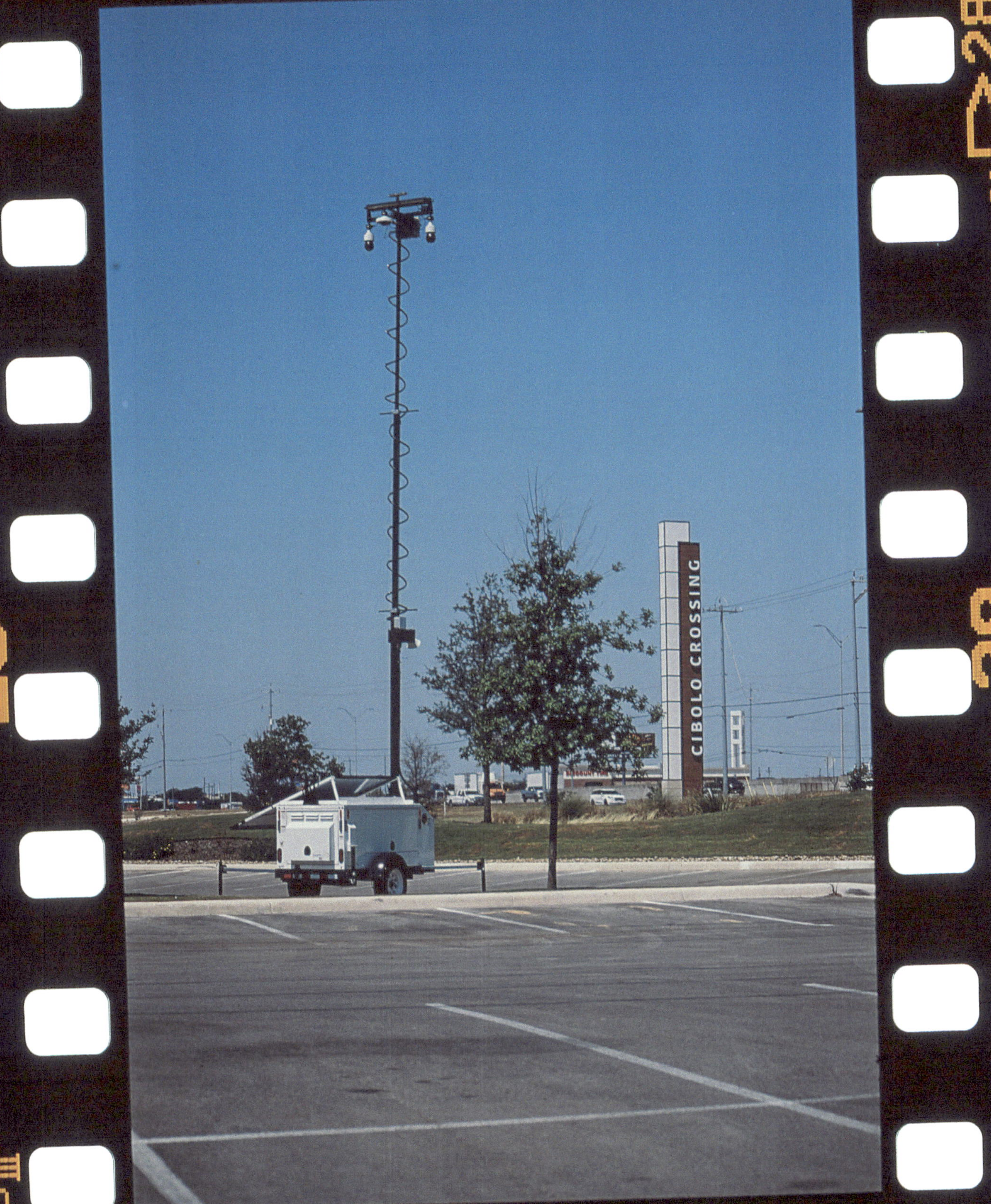
CIBOLO CROSSING

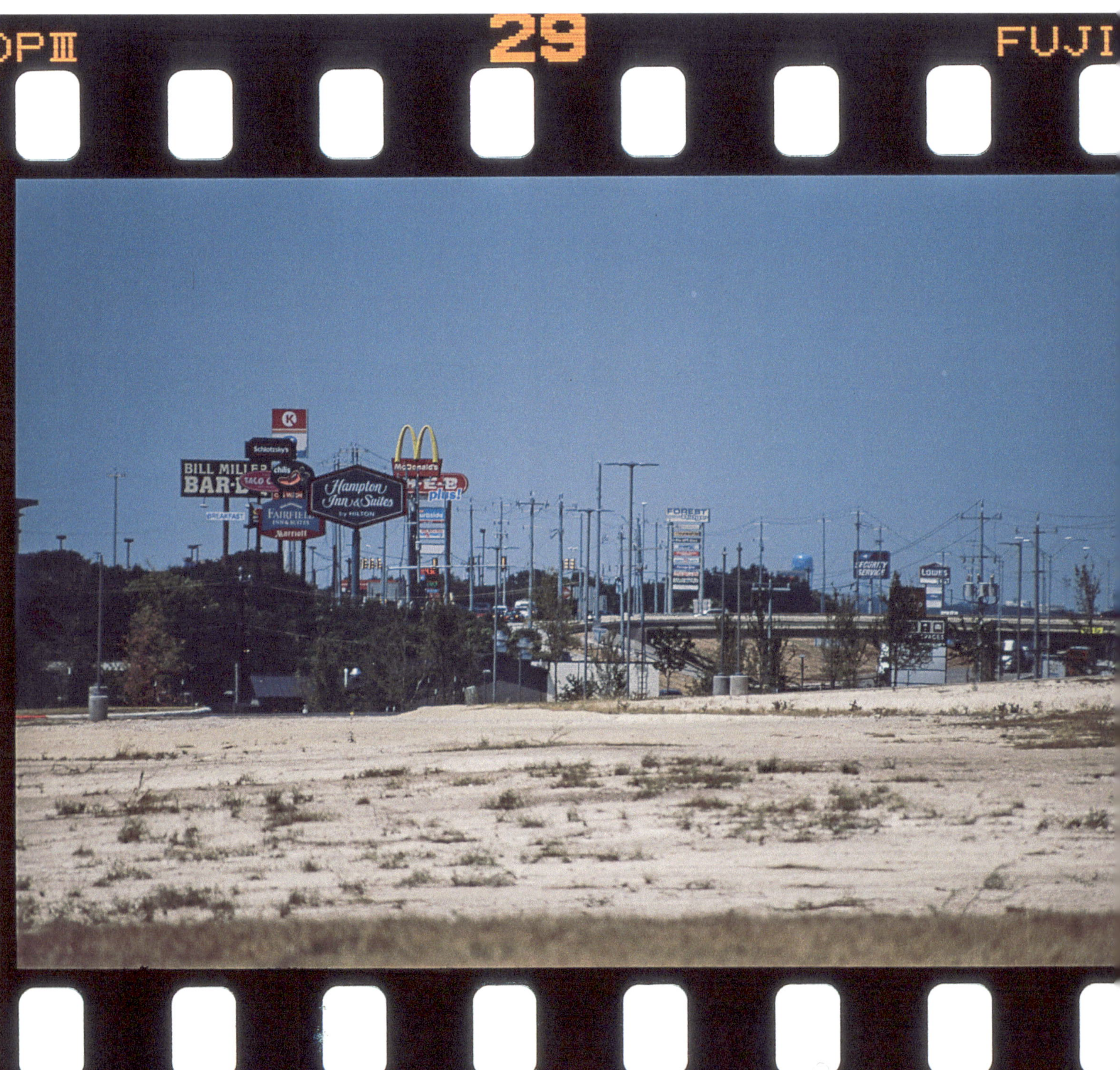
K
Schlotzsky's
BILL MILLER
BAR-B-Q
chili's
TACO C
BREAKFAST
Hampton
Inn & Suites
by HILTON
FAIRFIELD
INN & SUITES
Marriott
McDonald's
H-E-B
plus!
Curbside
FOREST
SECURITY
SERVICE
LOWE'S

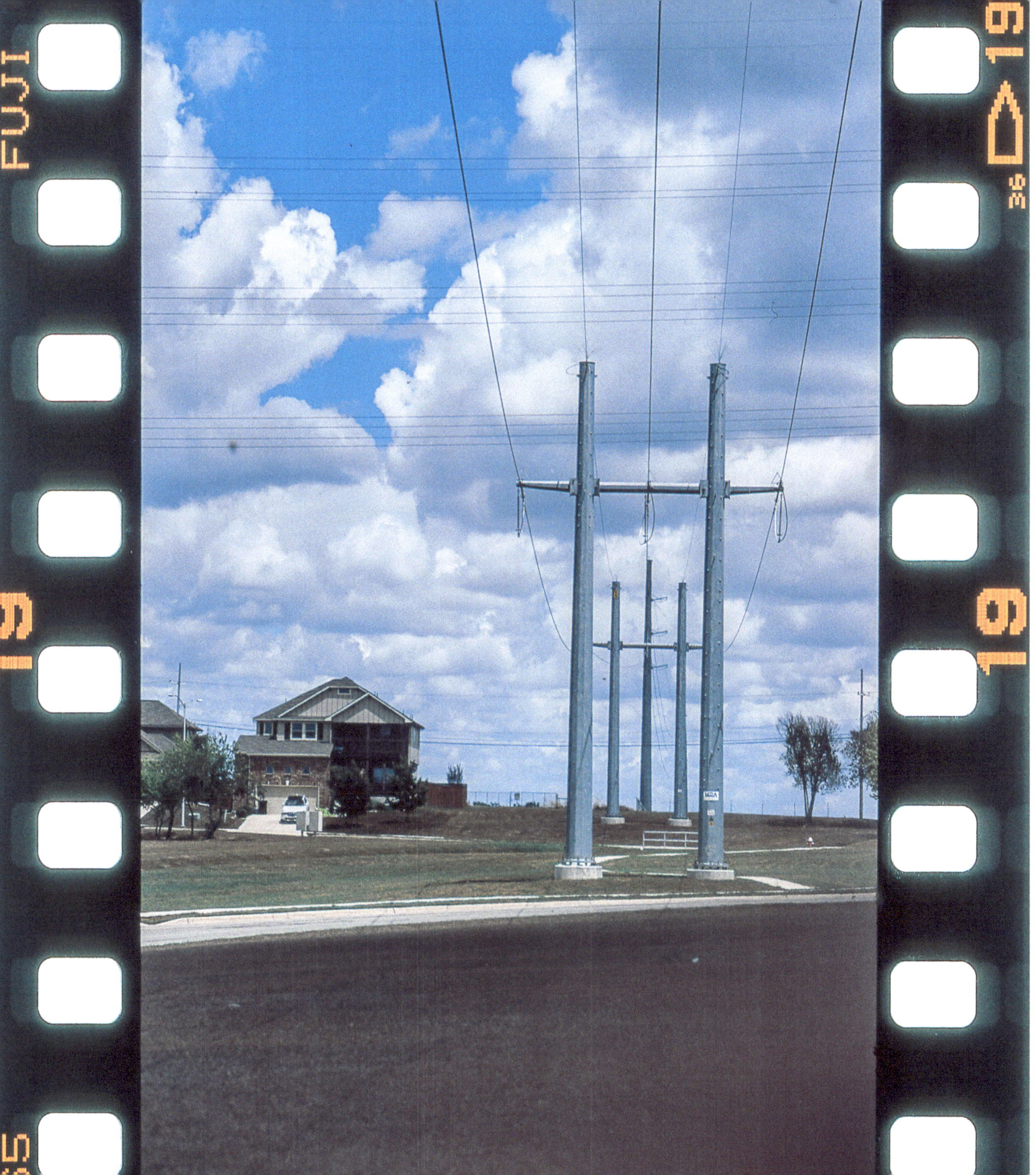

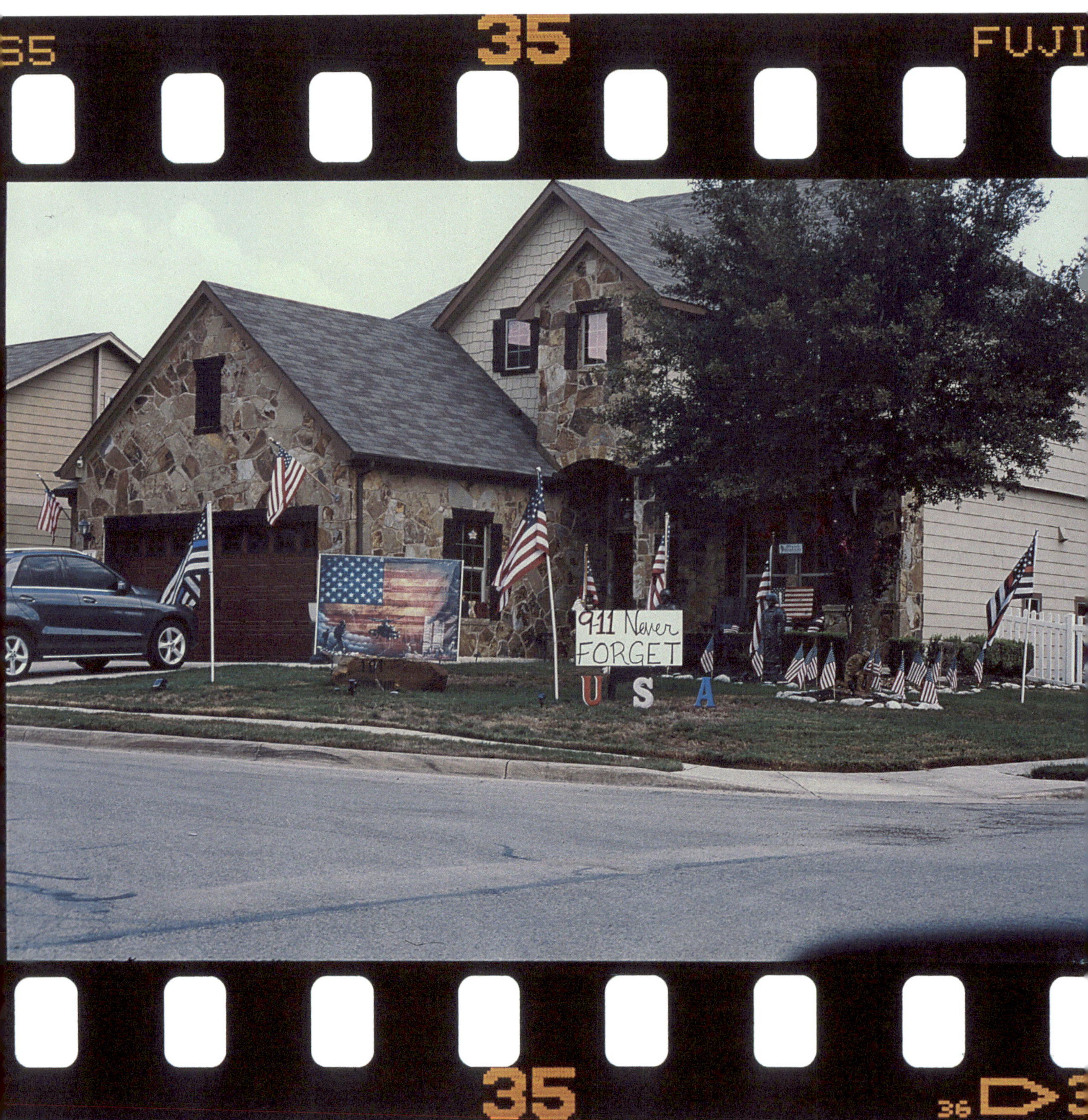
9-11 Never
FORGET
U S A

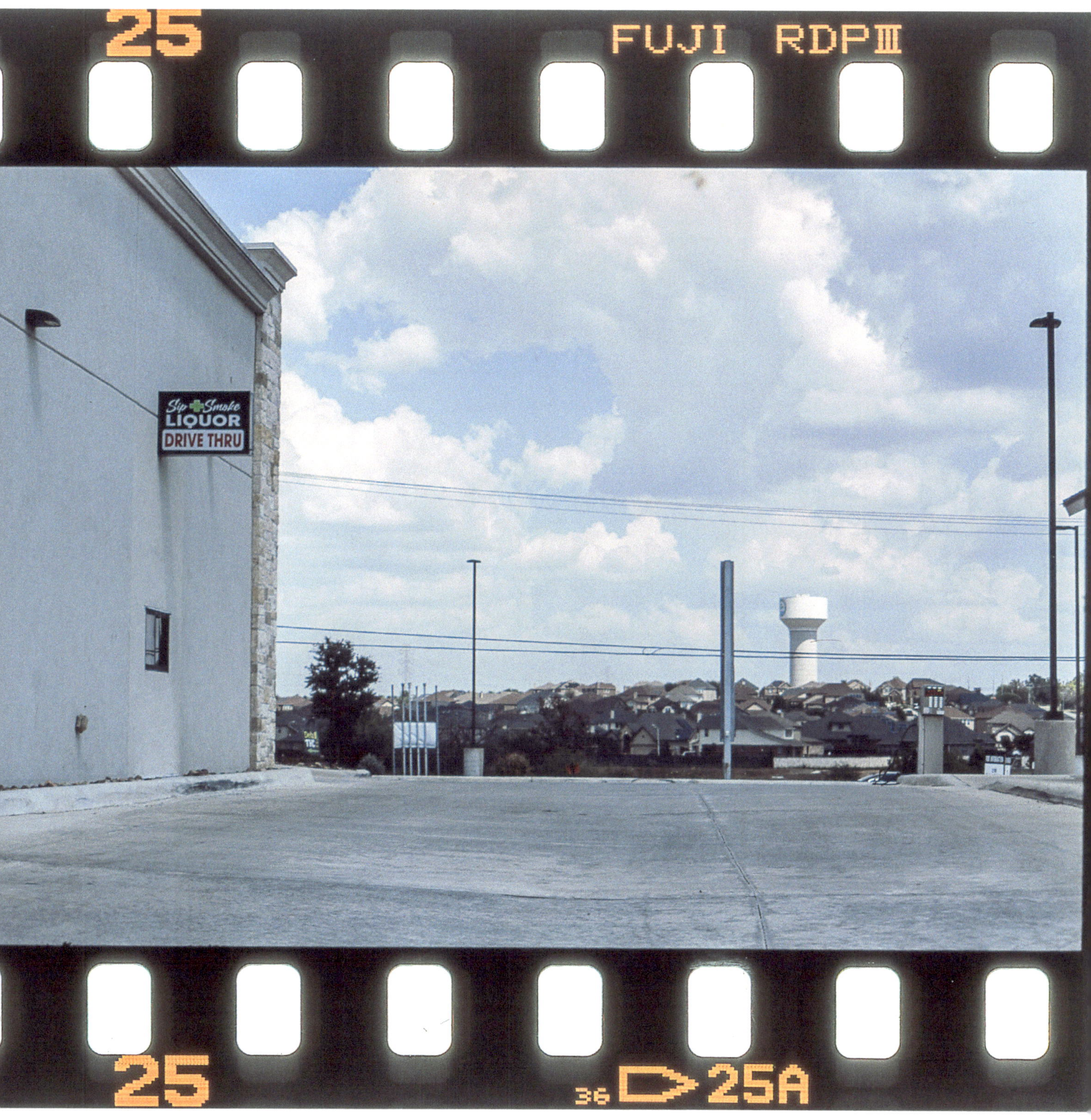
25
FUJI RDPIII
Sip Smoke
LIQUOR
DRIVE THRU
25
36 25A

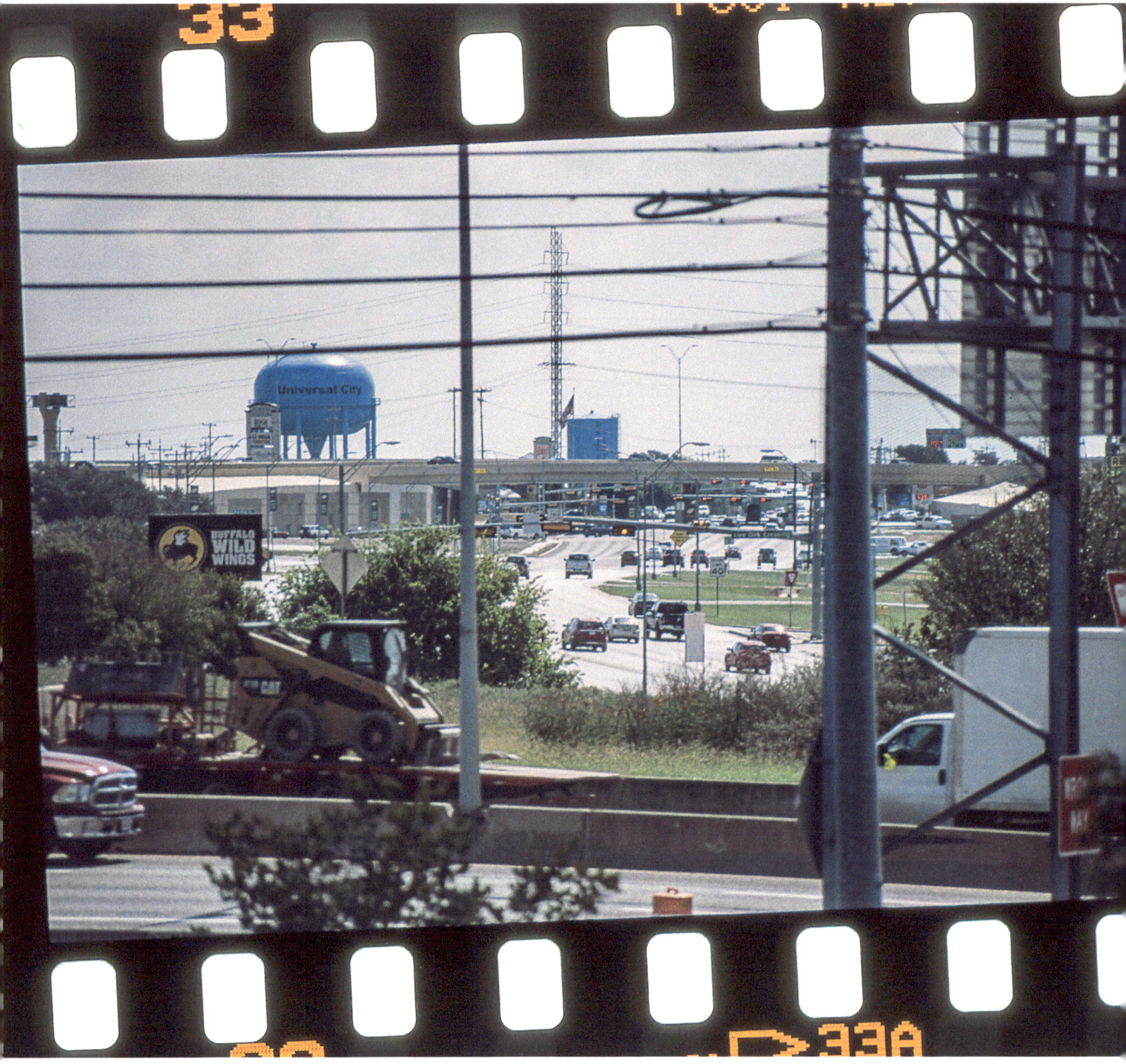
33
Universal City
BUFFALO WILD WINGS
Live Oak Crossing
40
33A

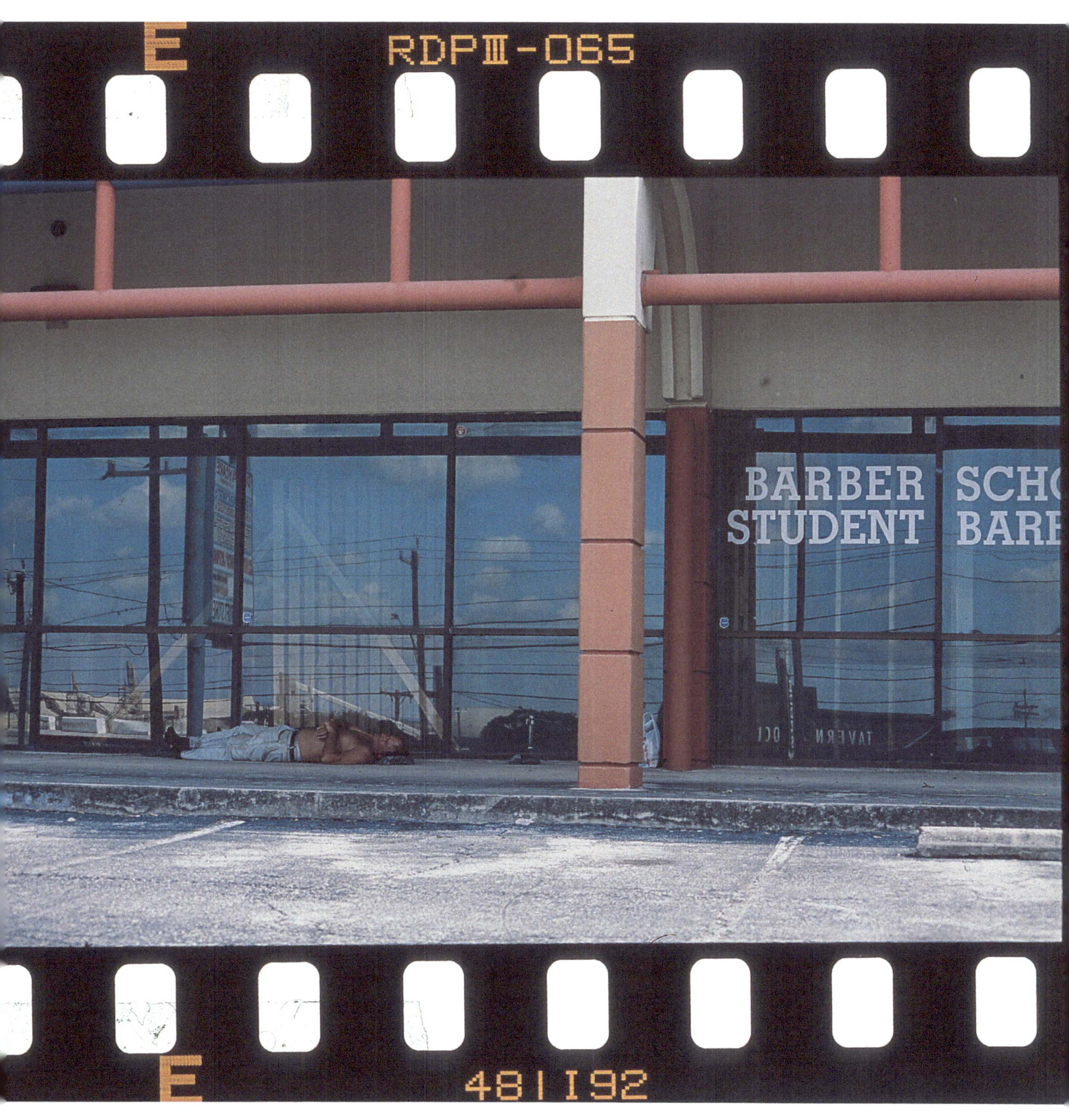
RDPⅢ-065
BARBER SCHO
STUDENT BARB
481 192

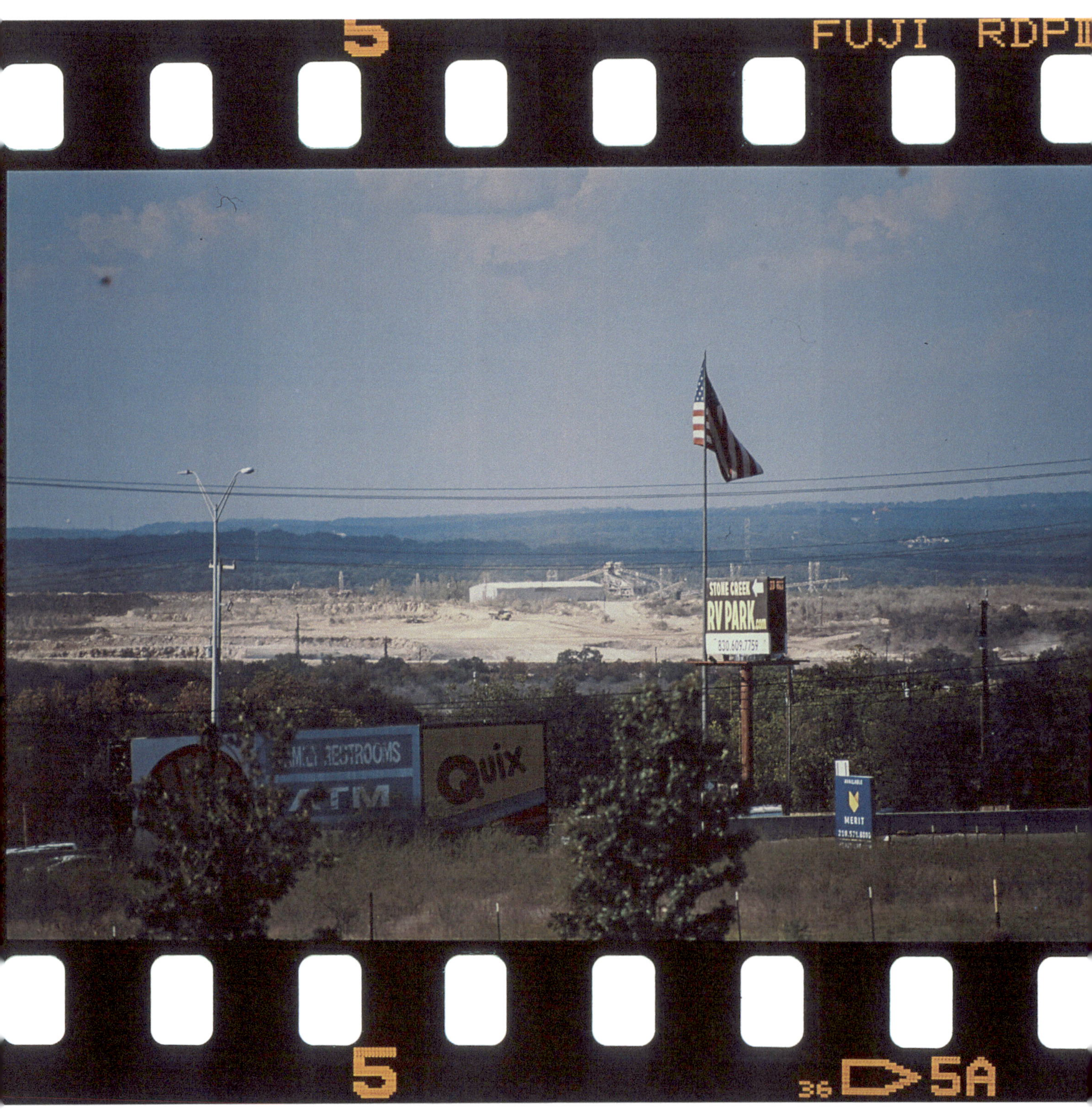
STONE CREEK
RV PARK
.com
830.609.7759
RESTROOMS
Quix
MERIT
FUJI RDP

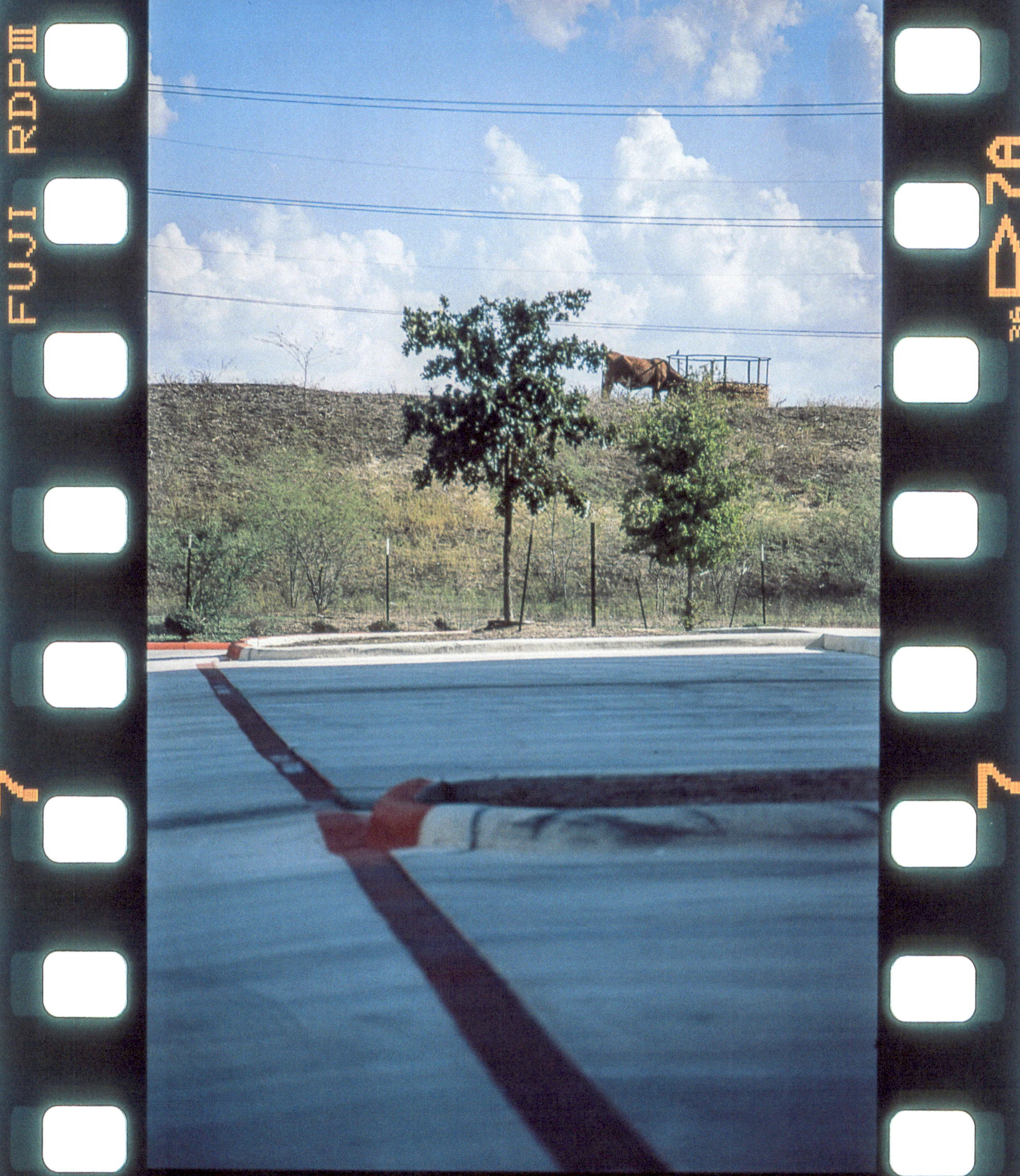
FUJI RDP III
36
D7A

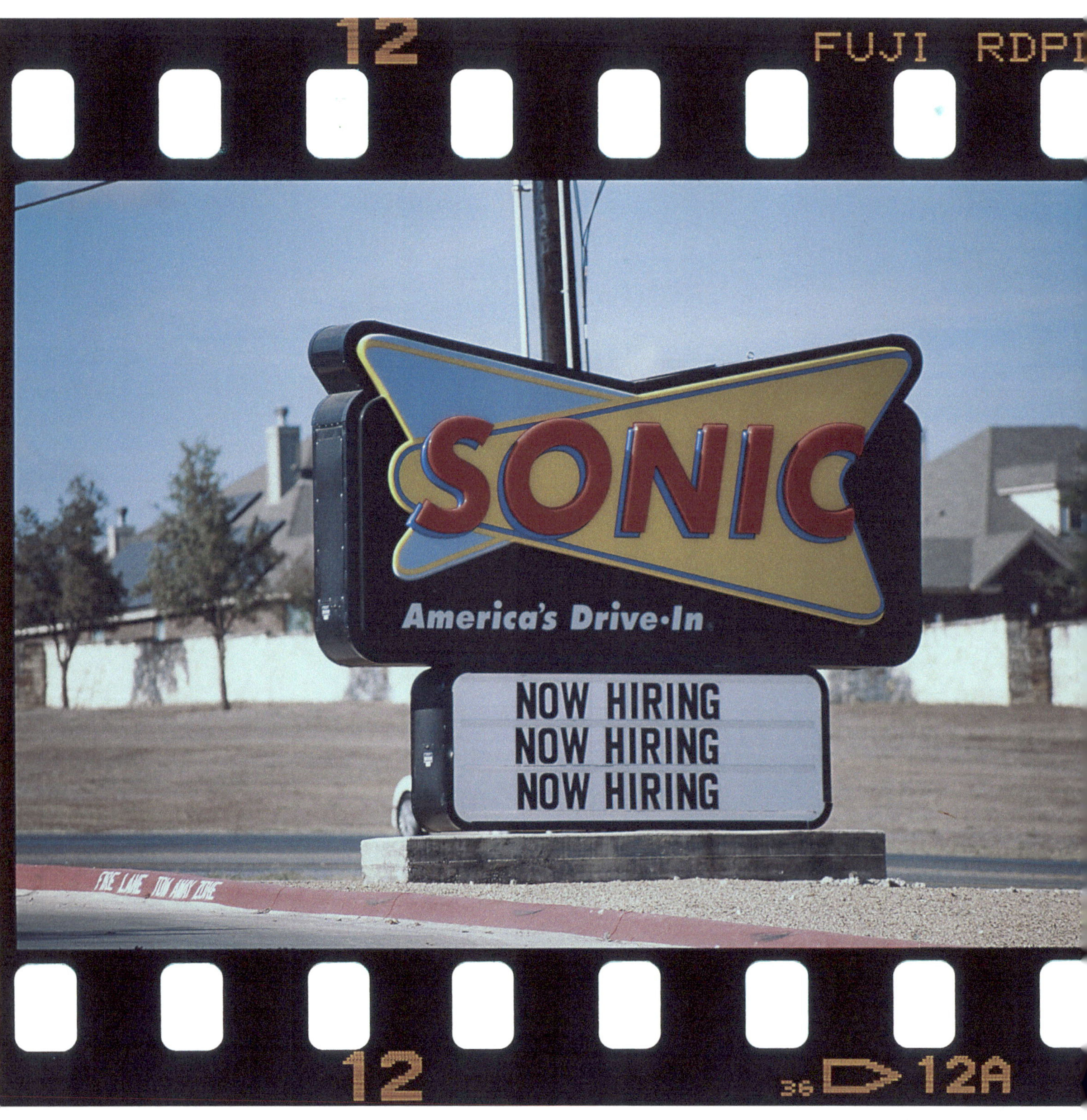
12
FUJI RDPI
SONIC
America's Drive·In
NOW HIRING
NOW HIRING
NOW HIRING
12
36
12A

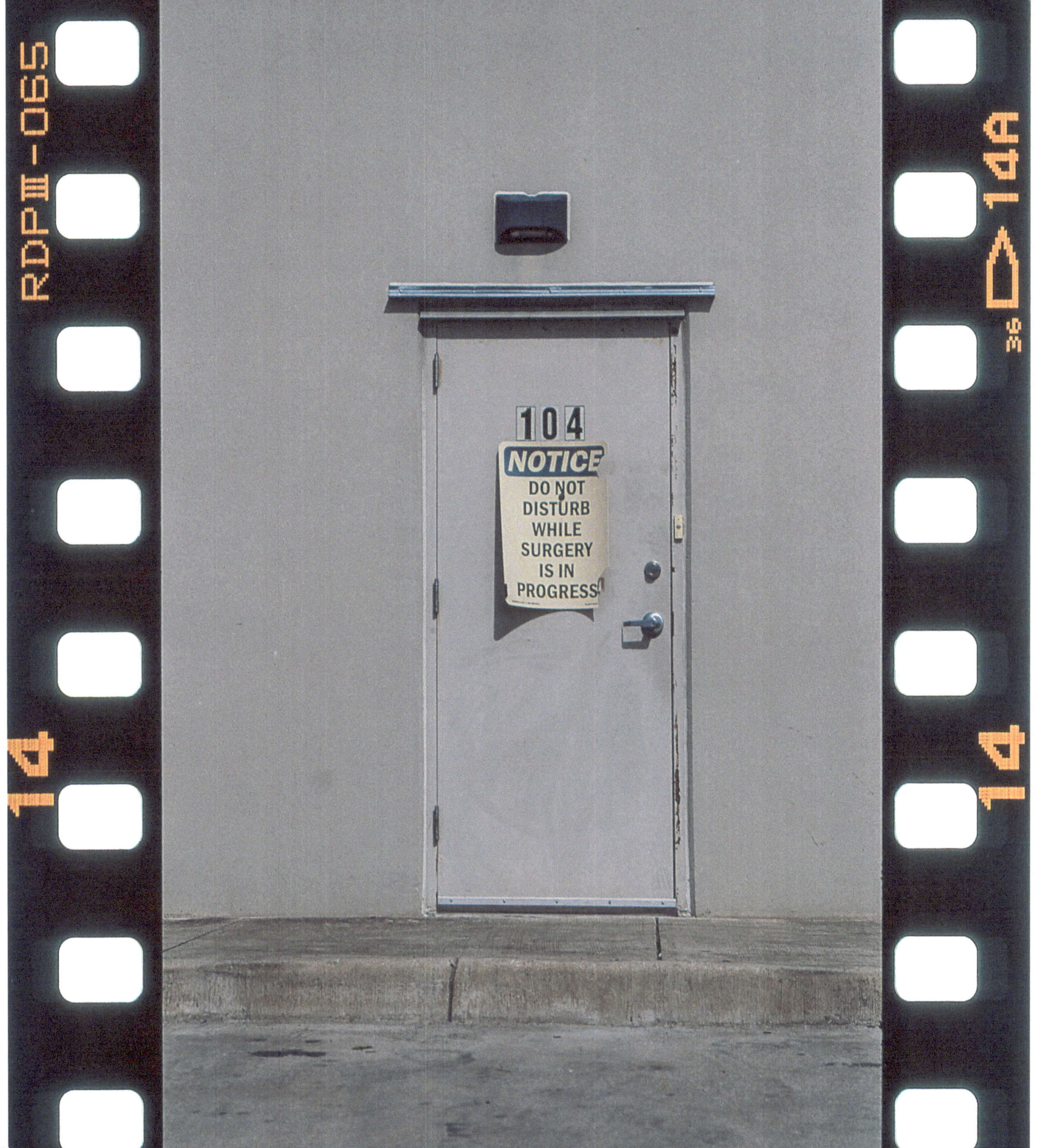

104
NOTICE
DO NOT
DISTURB
WHILE
SURGERY
IS IN
PROGRESS

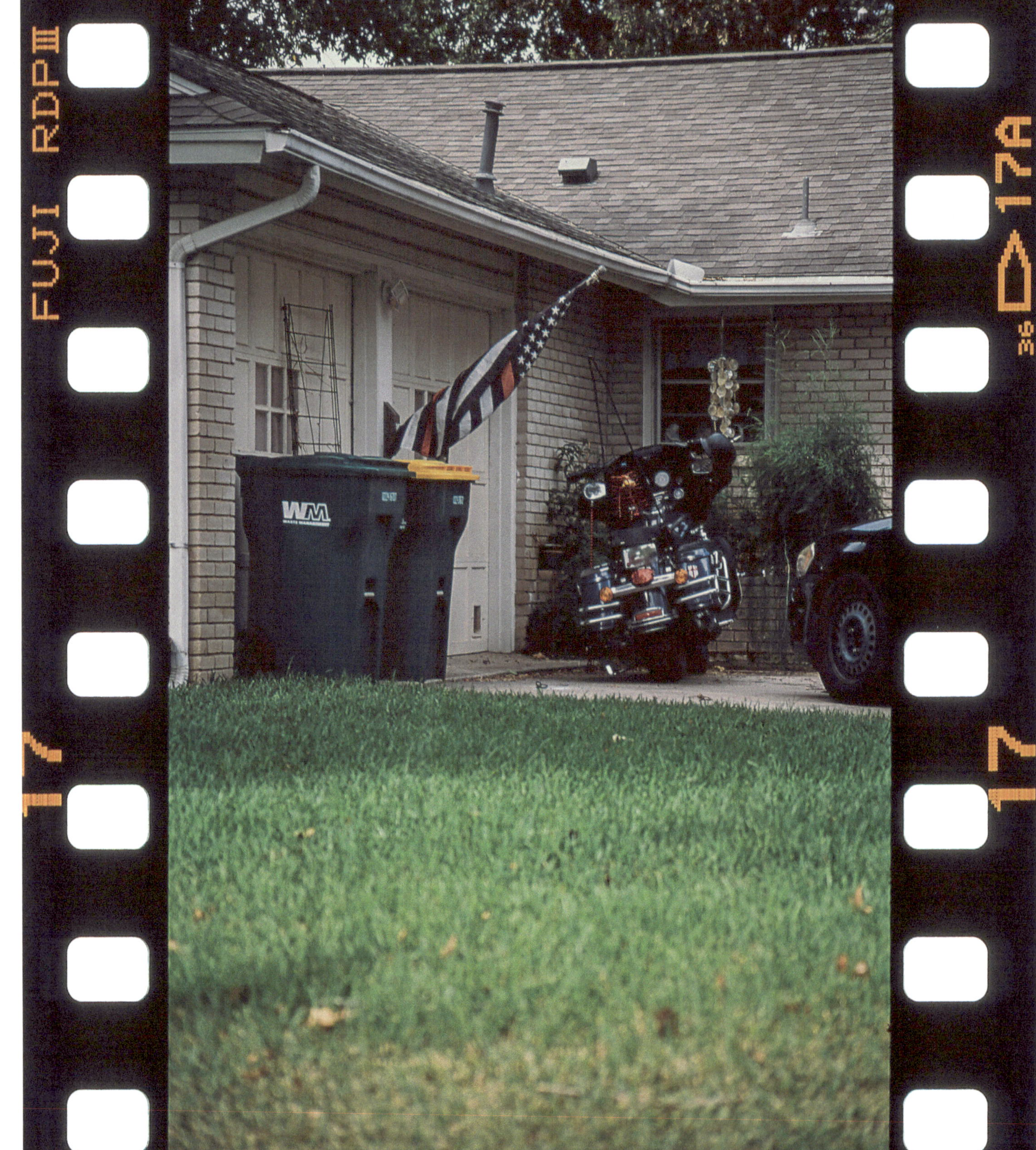

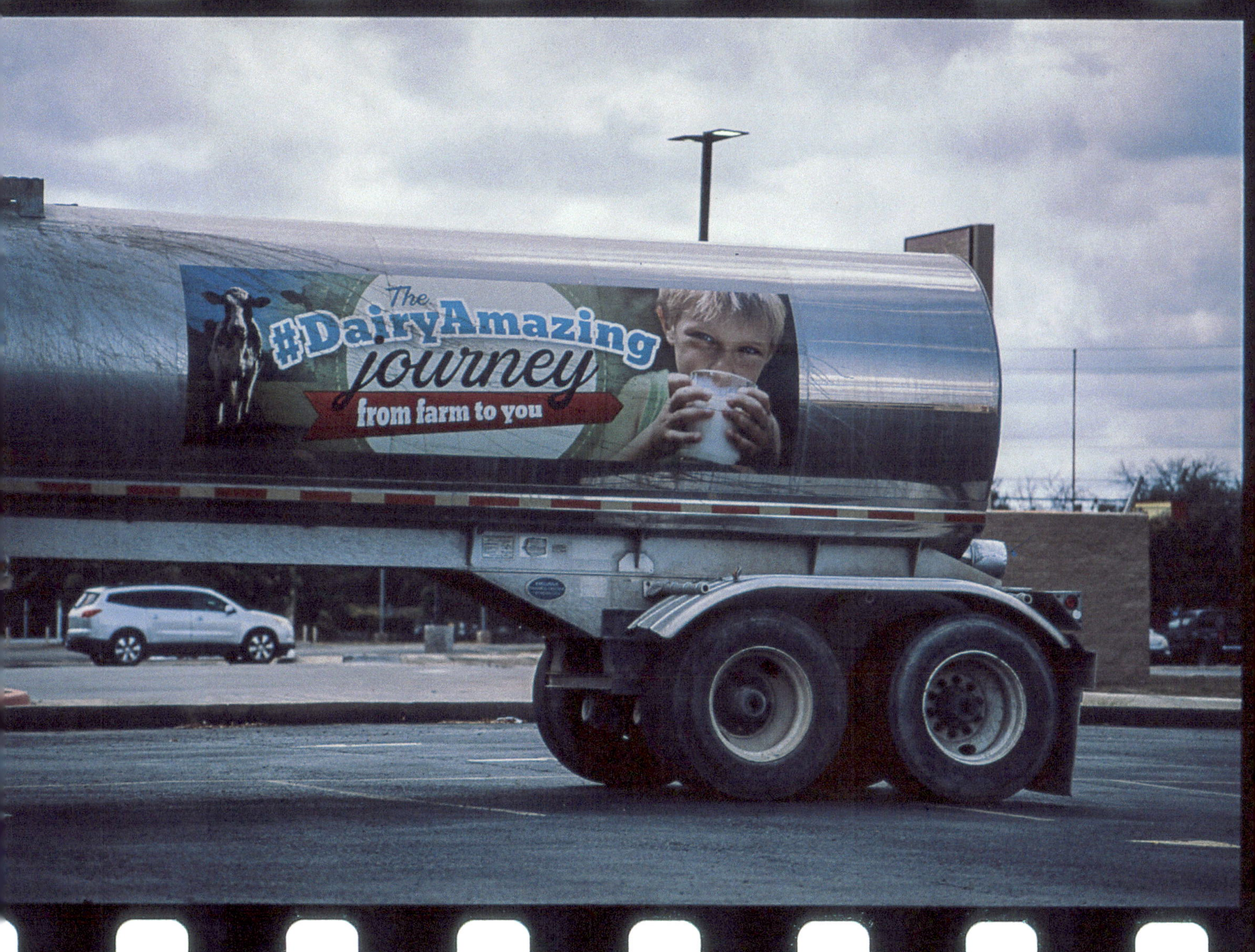

The #DairyAmazing
journey
from farm to you
29
FUJI RDPIII
29
36 29A

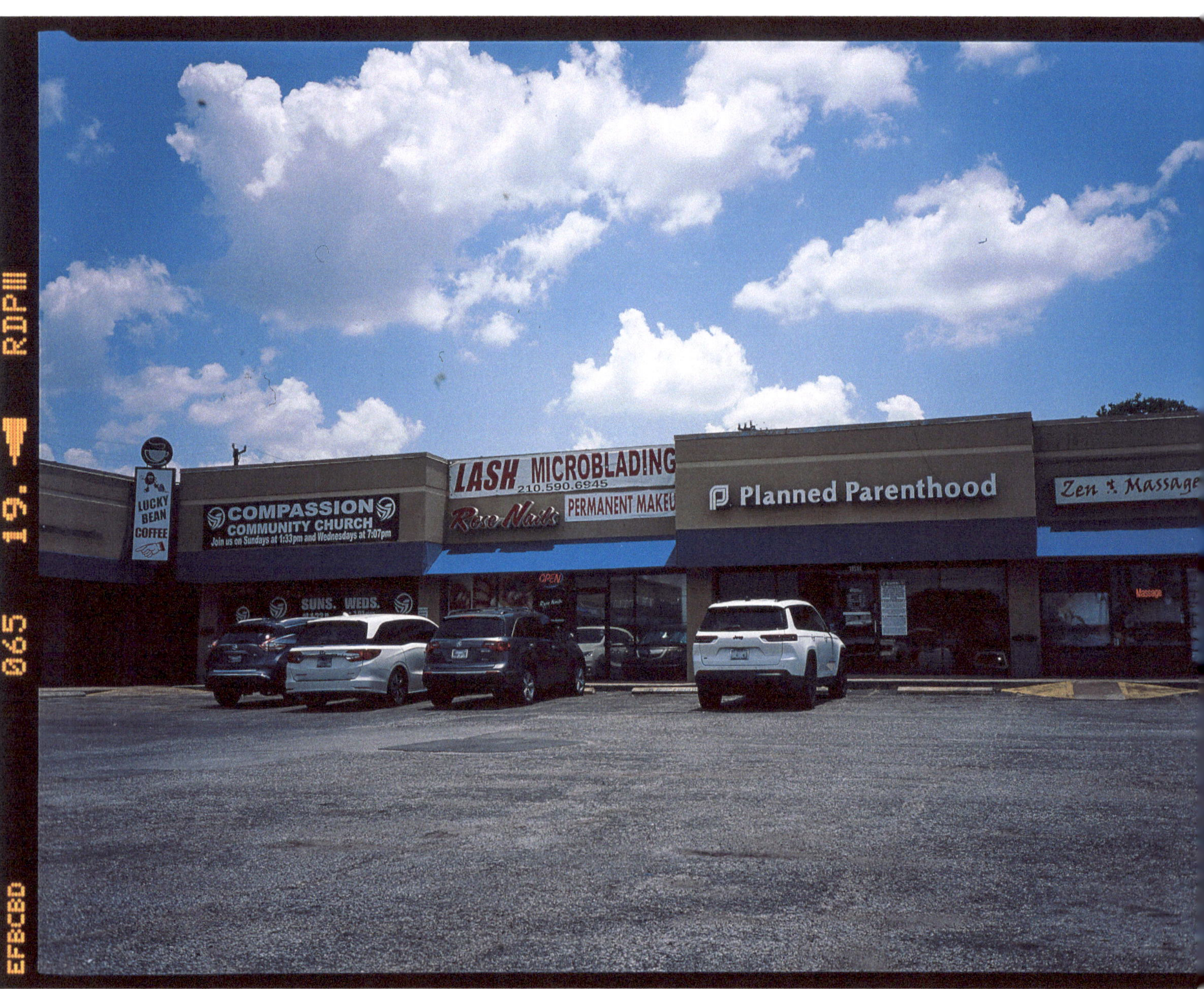
LUCKY BEAN COFFEE
COMPASSION COMMUNITY CHURCH
Join us on Sundays at 1:33pm and Wednesdays at 7:07pm
LASH MICROBLADING
210.590.6945
Rose Nails
PERMANENT MAKEUP
OPEN
SUNS. WEDS.
Planned Parenthood
Zen Massage
Massage

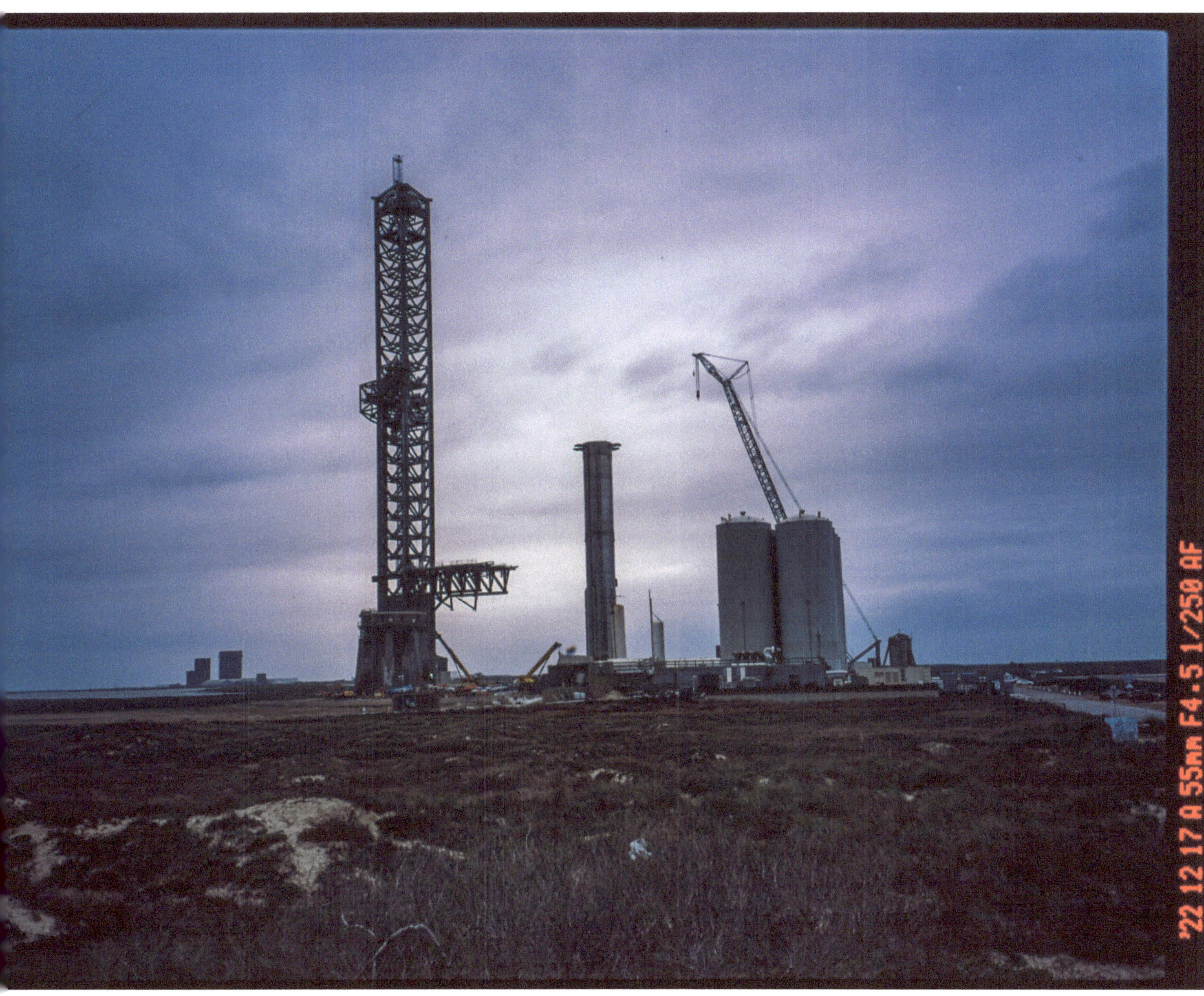
'22 12 17 A 55mm F4・5 1/250 AF

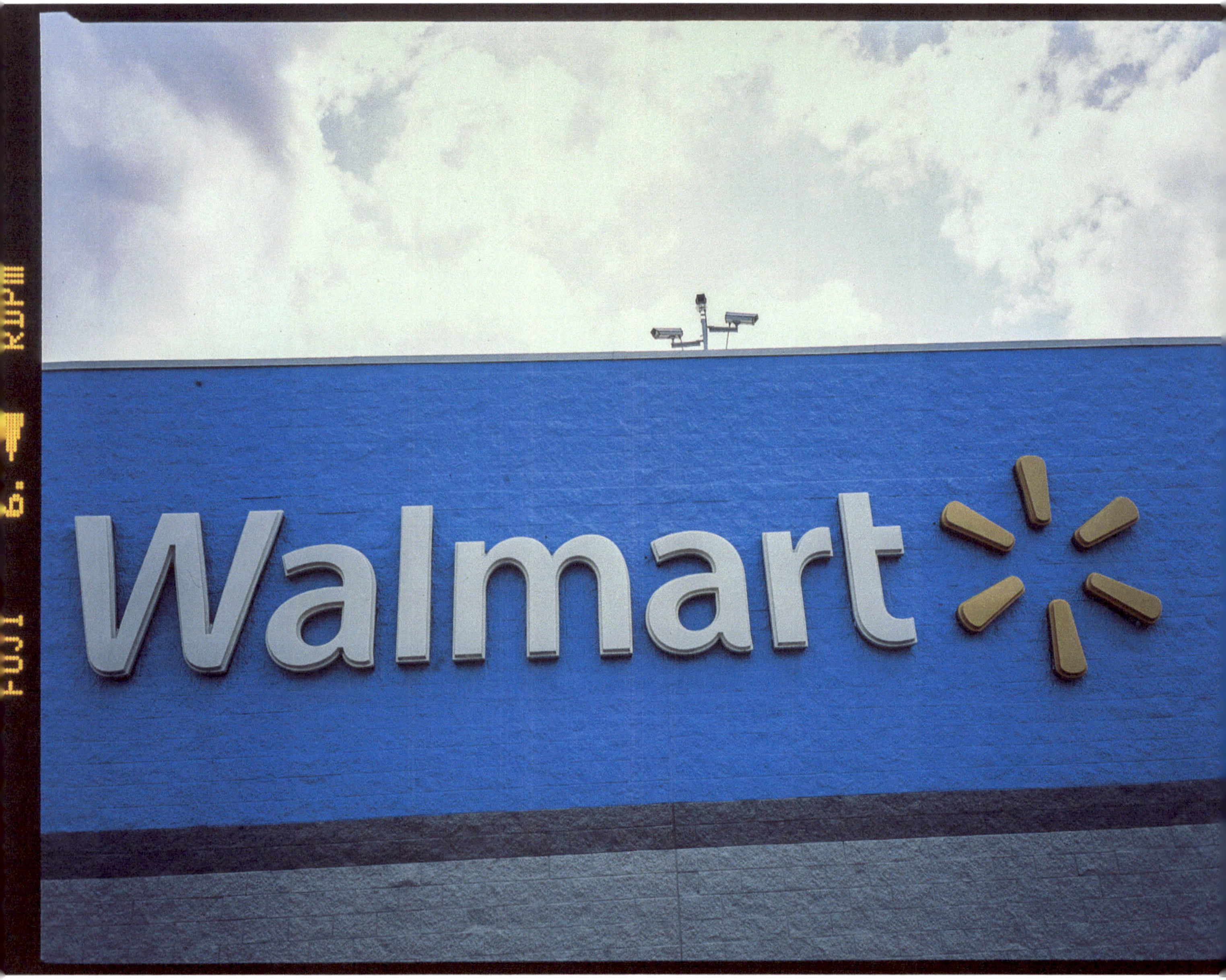

Walmart

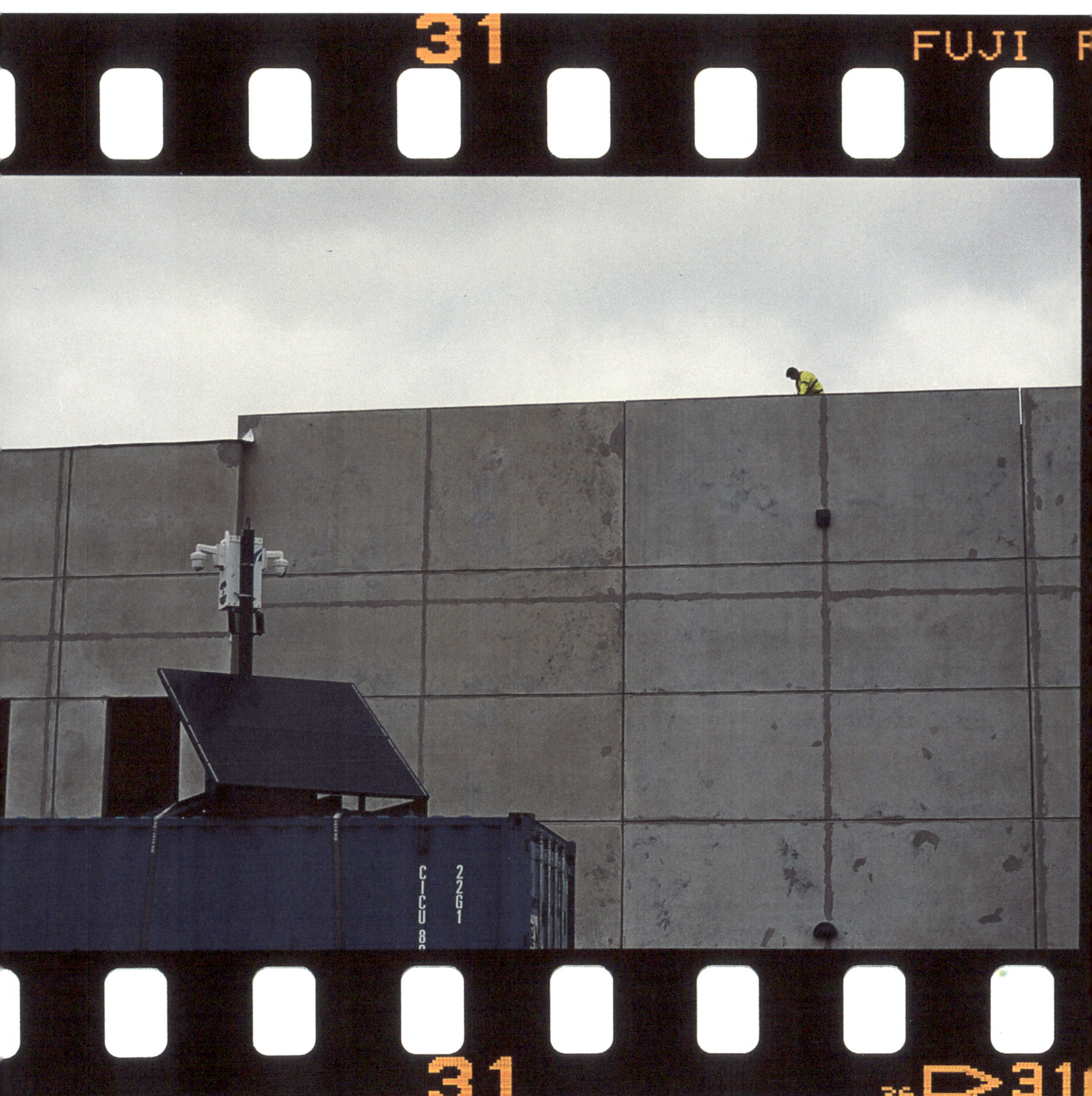
31
FUJI
CICU 8
22G1
31
36
31

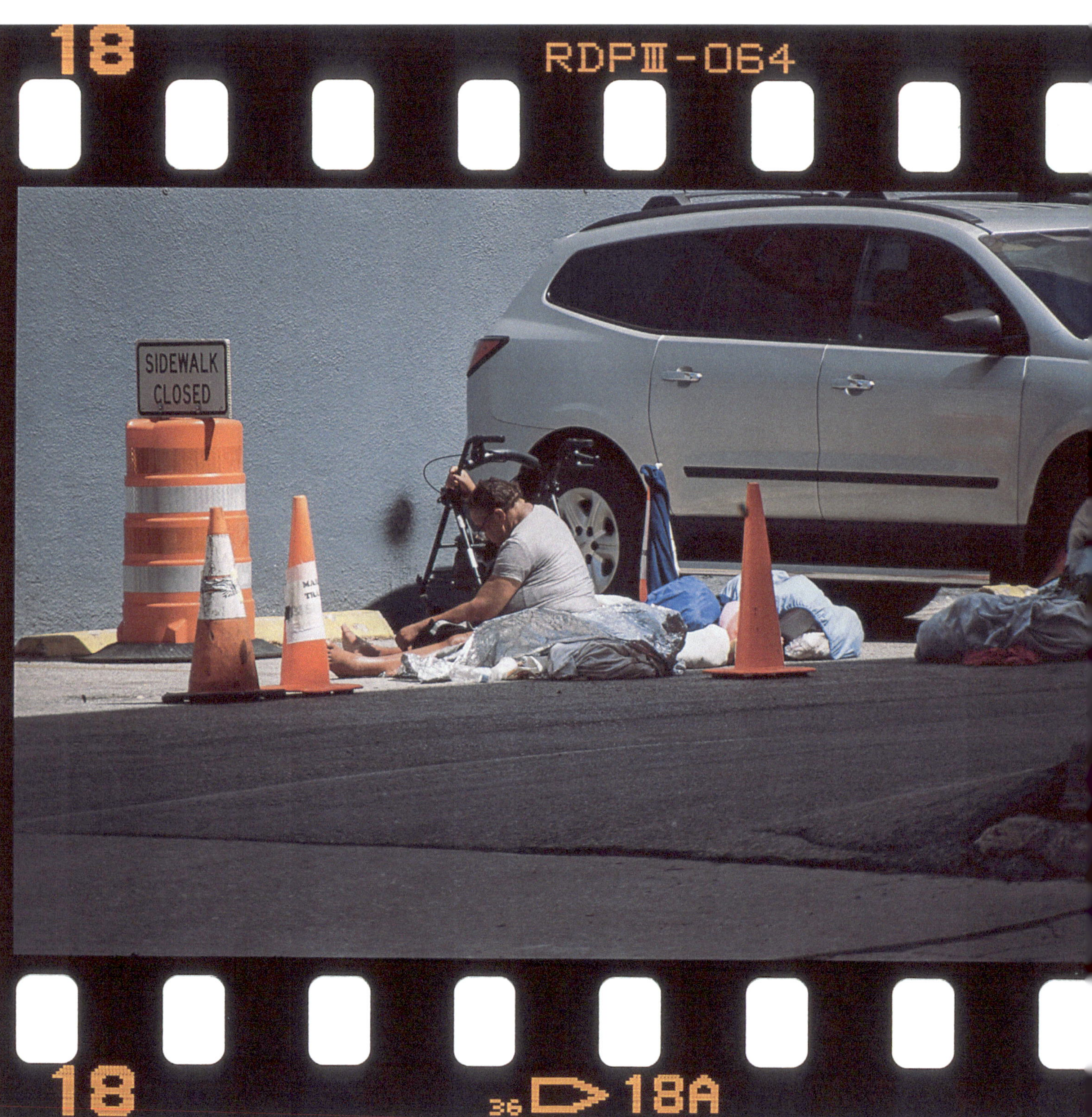
SIDEWALK CLOSED

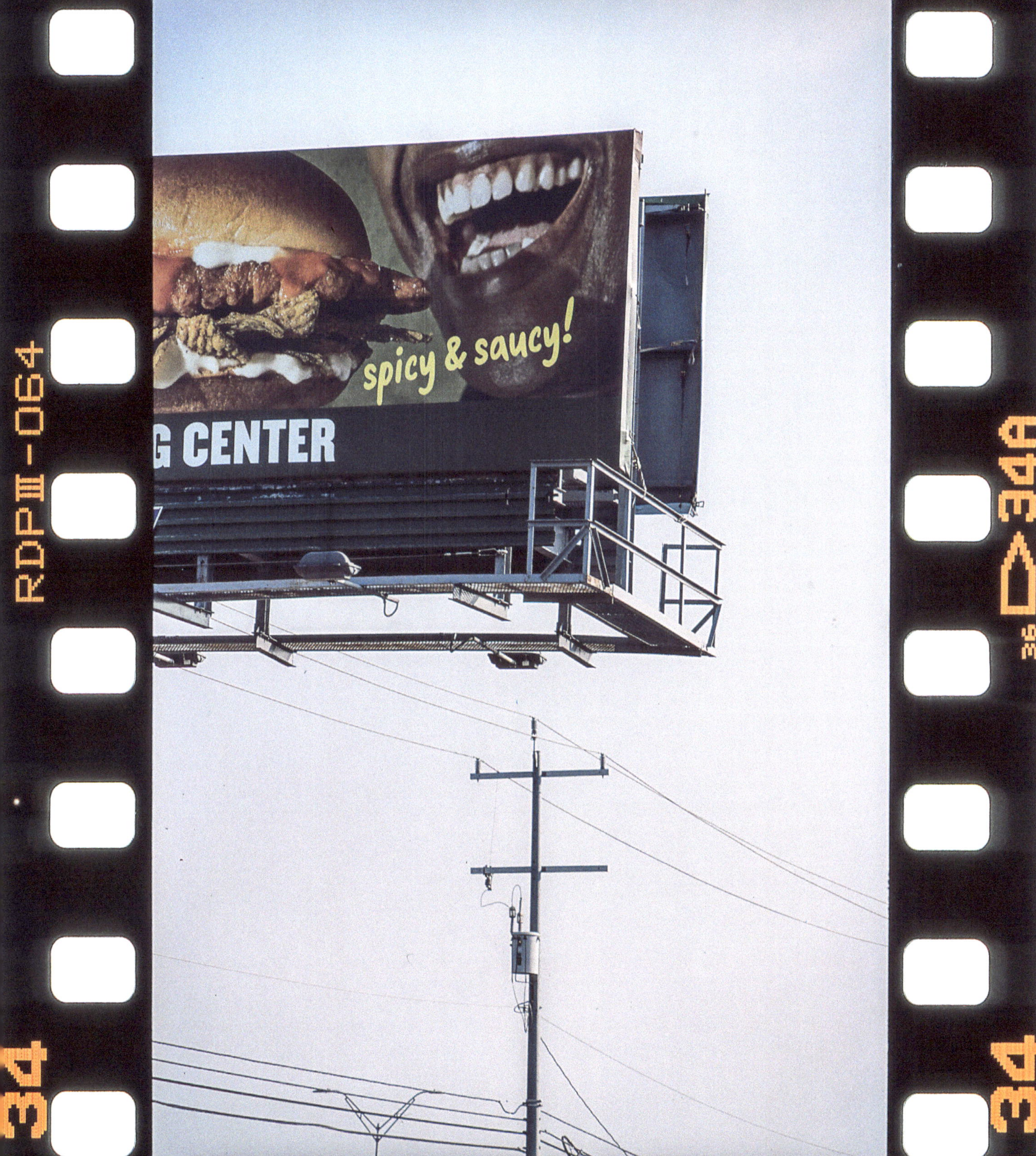

spicy & saucy!
G CENTER
RDP III–064
34A
36
34
34

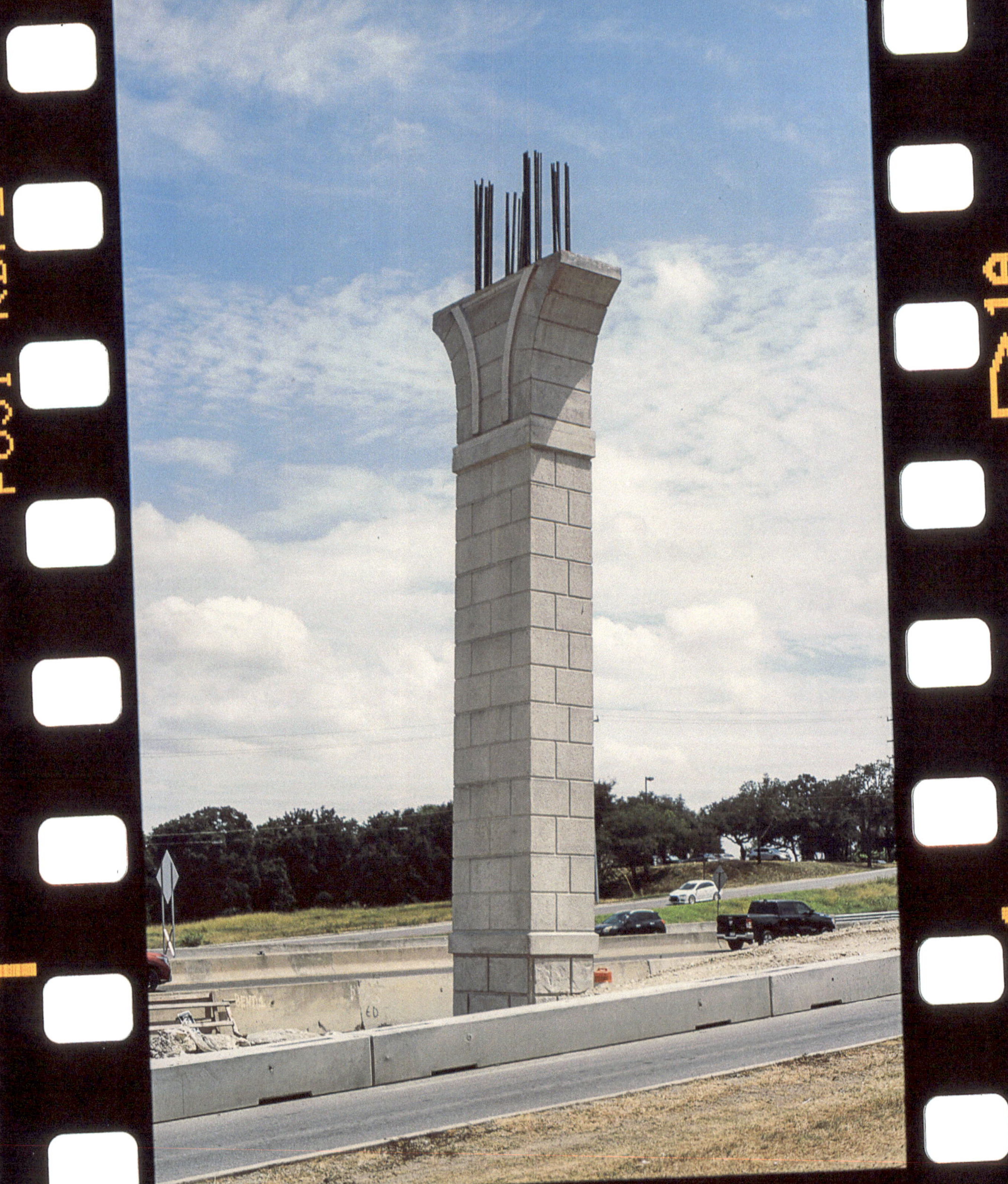

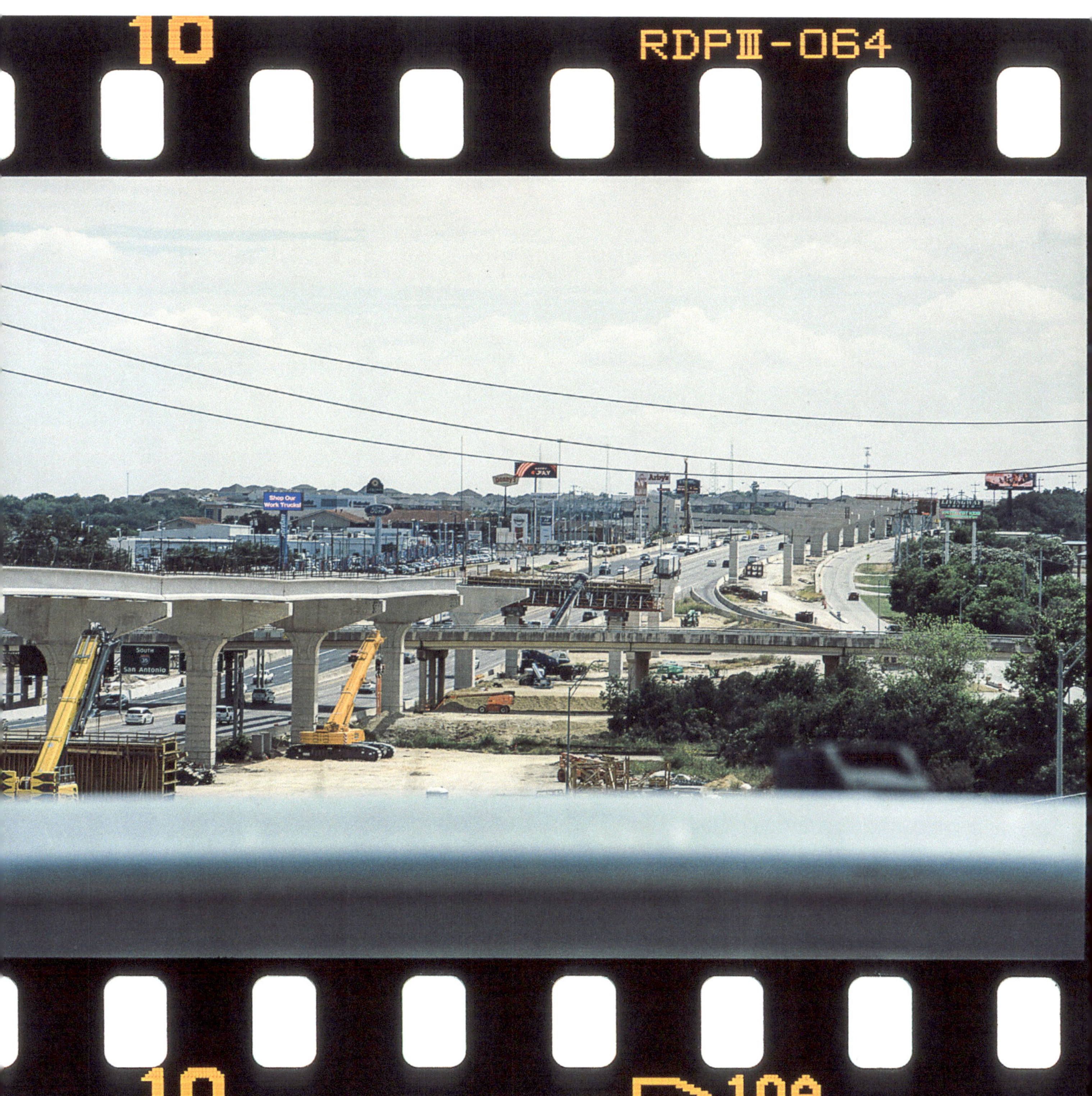

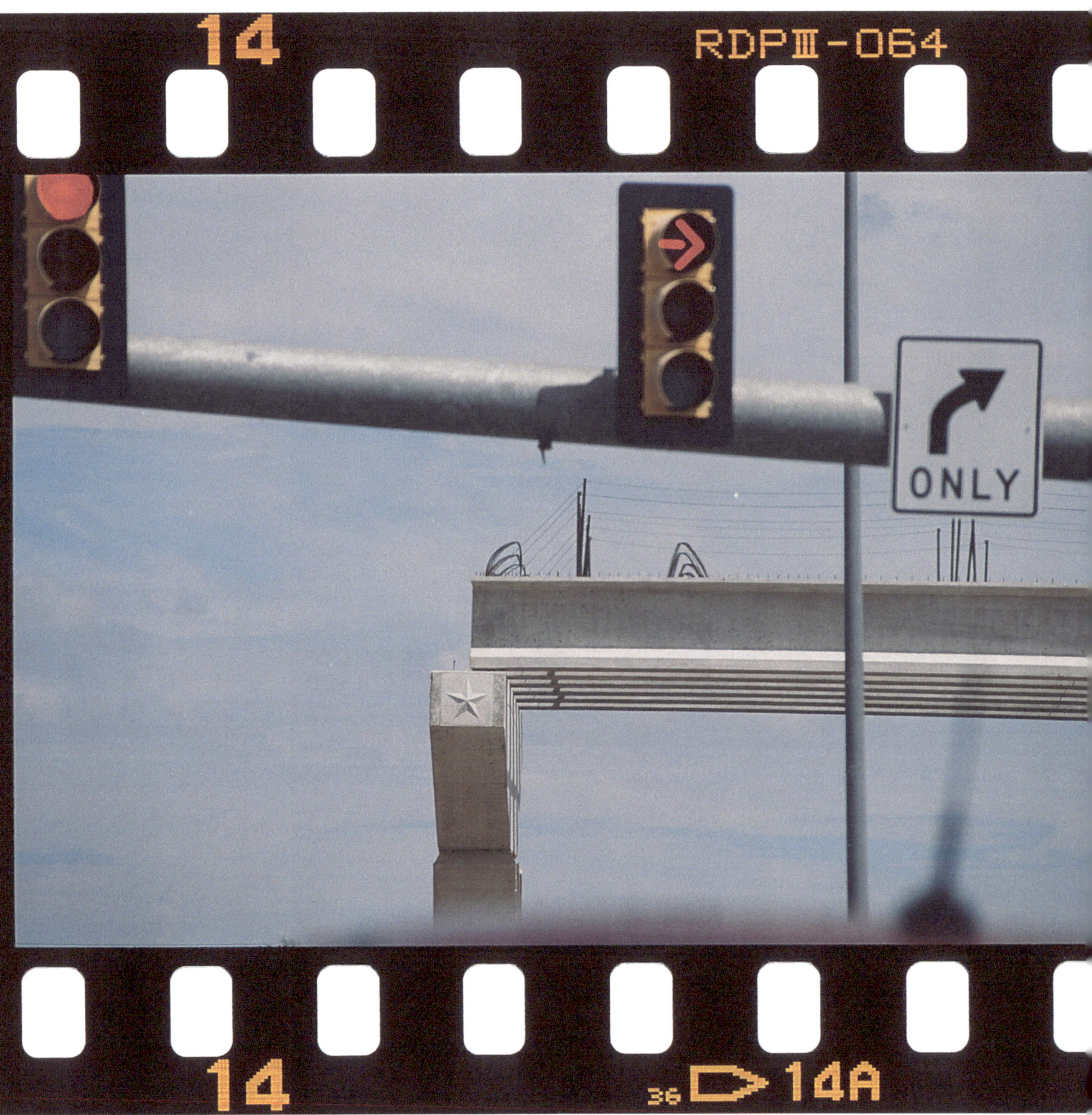
ONLY

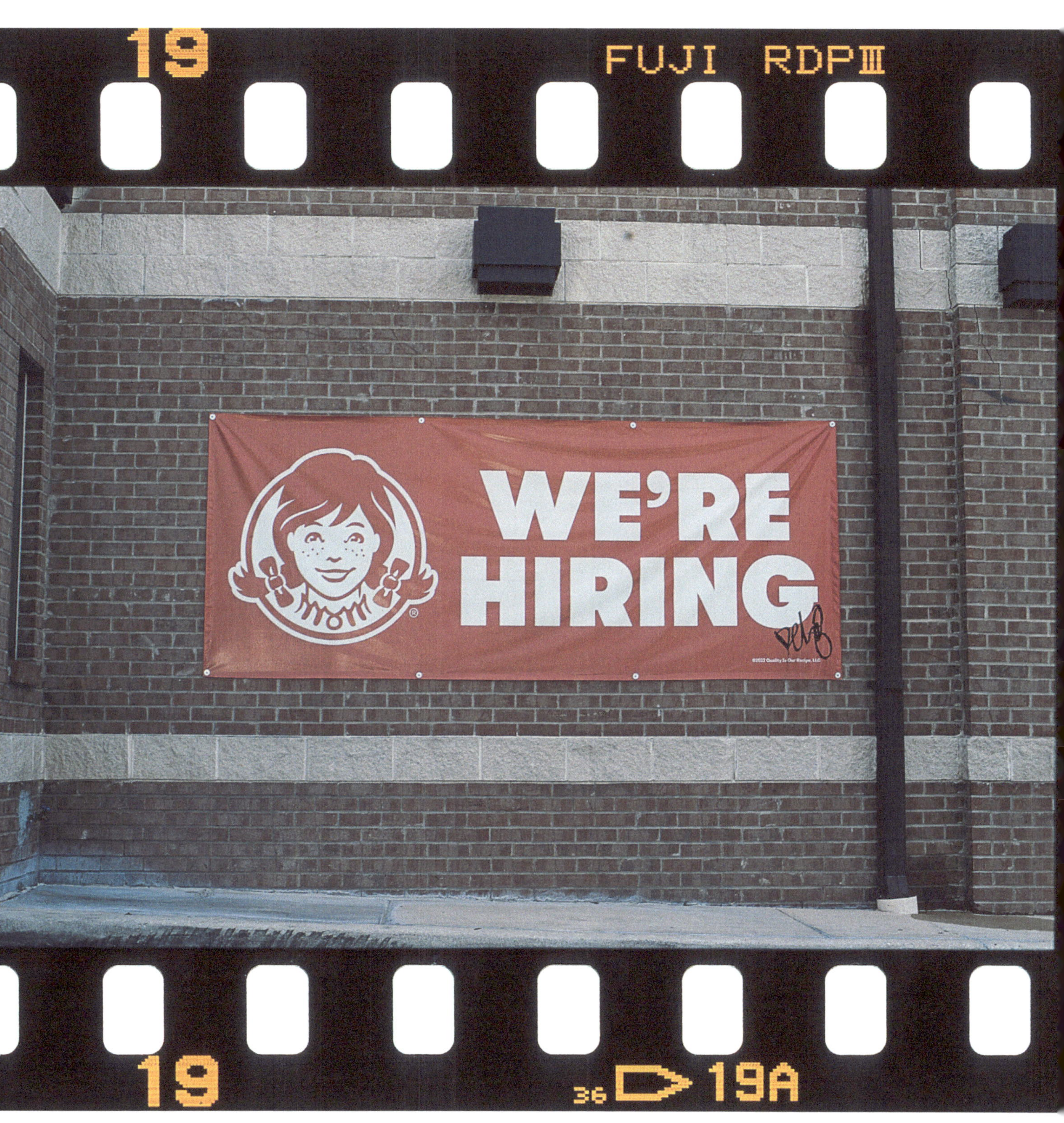

19
FUJI RDP III
WE'RE HIRING
19
36
19A

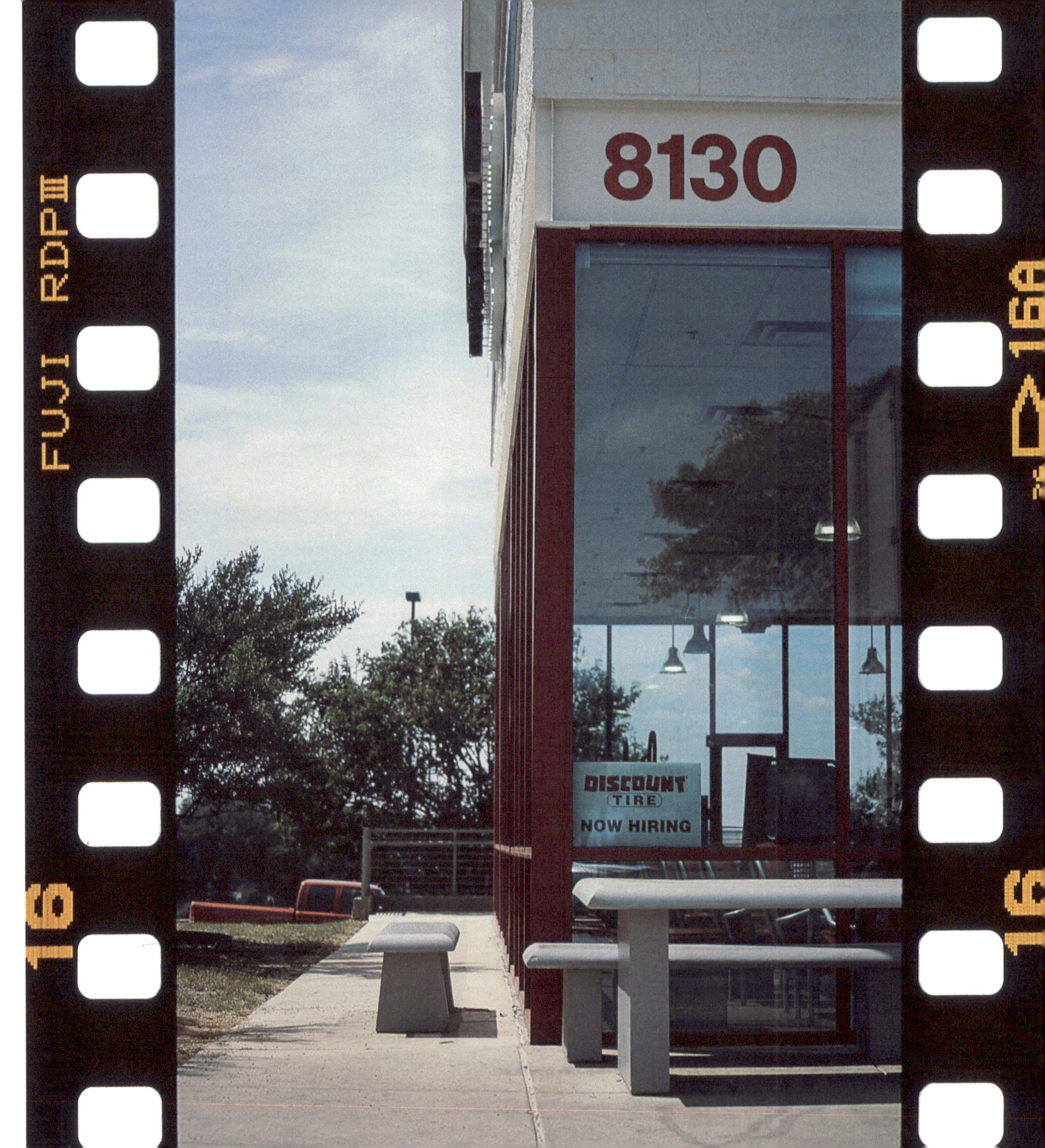

FUJI RDPⅢ
16
8130
DISCOUNT
TIRE
NOW HIRING

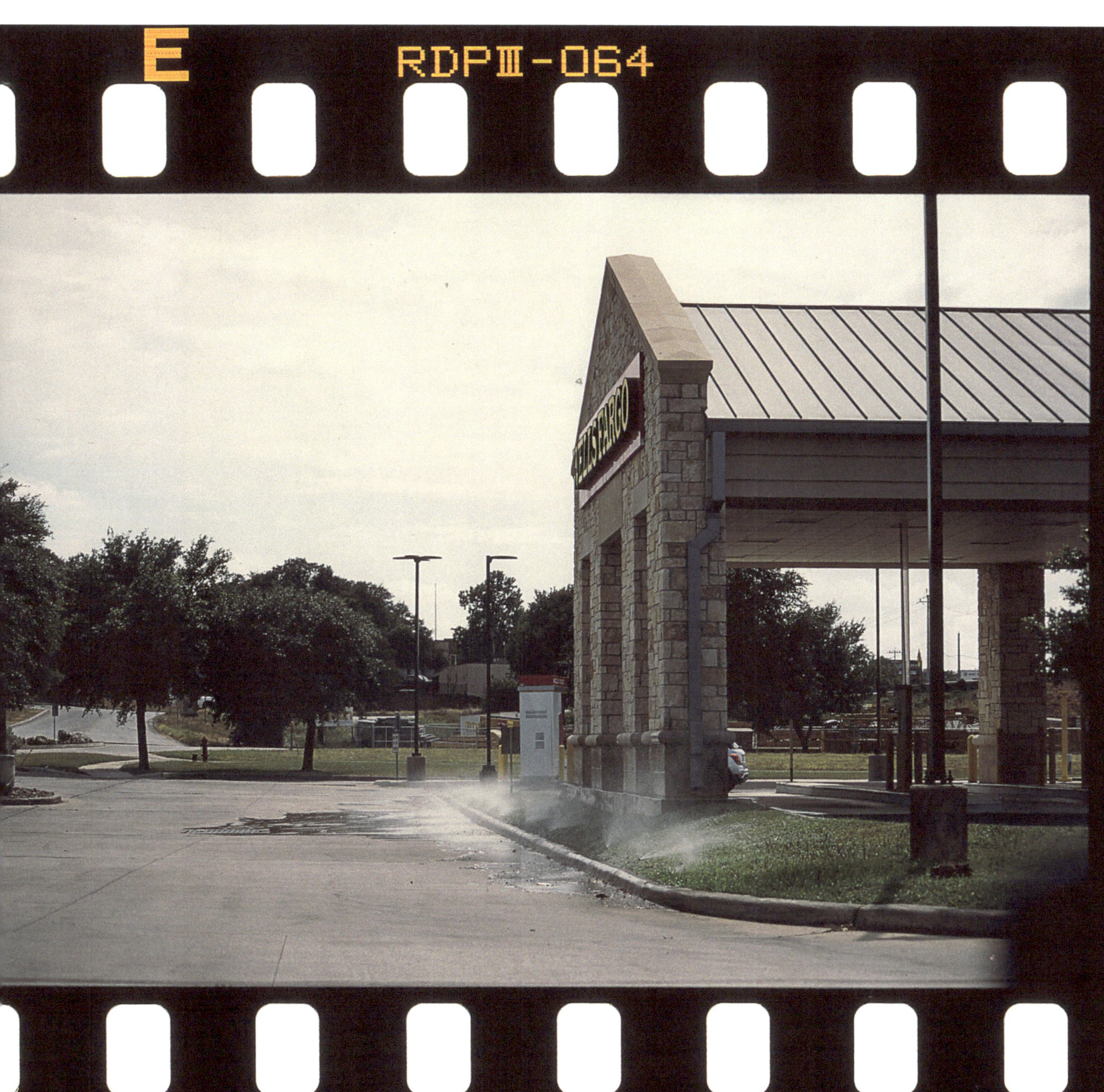
RDPⅢ-064
484222
WELLS FARGO

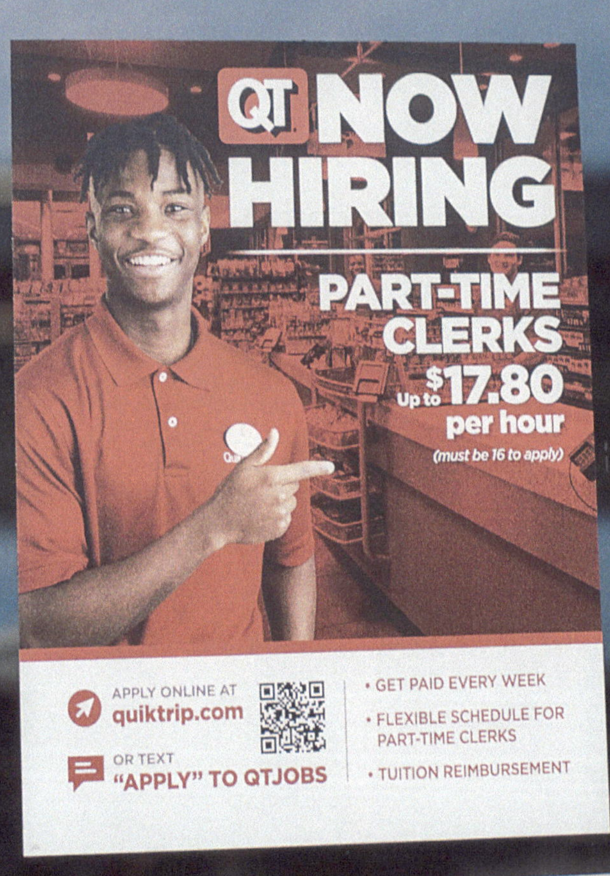
QT NOW HIRING
PART-TIME CLERKS
Up to $17.80 per hour
(must be 16 to apply)
APPLY ONLINE AT
quiktrip.com
OR TEXT
"APPLY" TO QTJOBS
• GET PAID EVERY WEEK
• FLEXIBLE SCHEDULE FOR PART-TIME CLERKS
• TUITION REIMBURSEMENT

roduct contains nicotine. Nicotine is an addictiv

Quality ingredients
blended in the U.S.A.

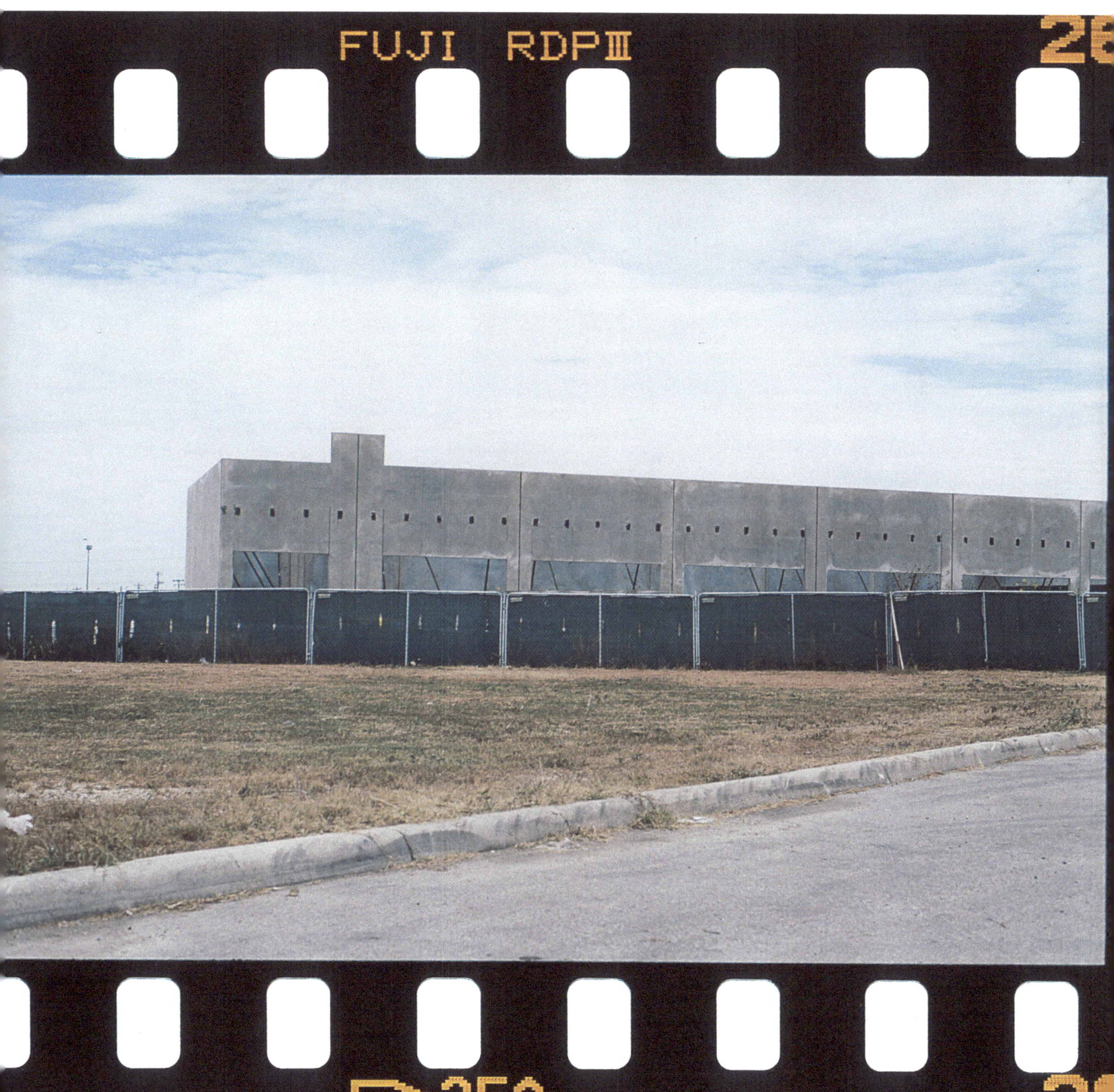

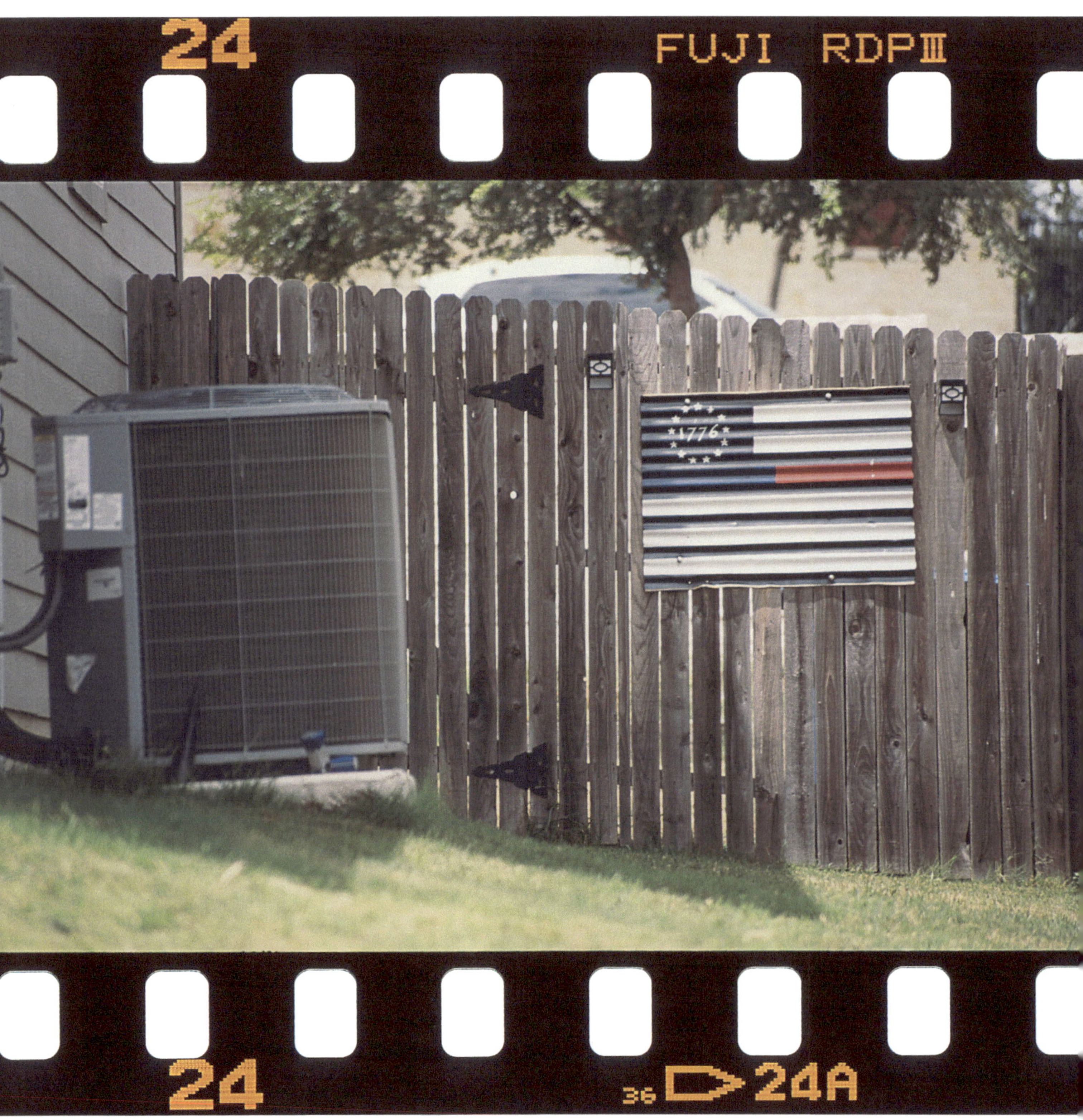
24
FUJI RDPⅢ
1776
24
36 24A

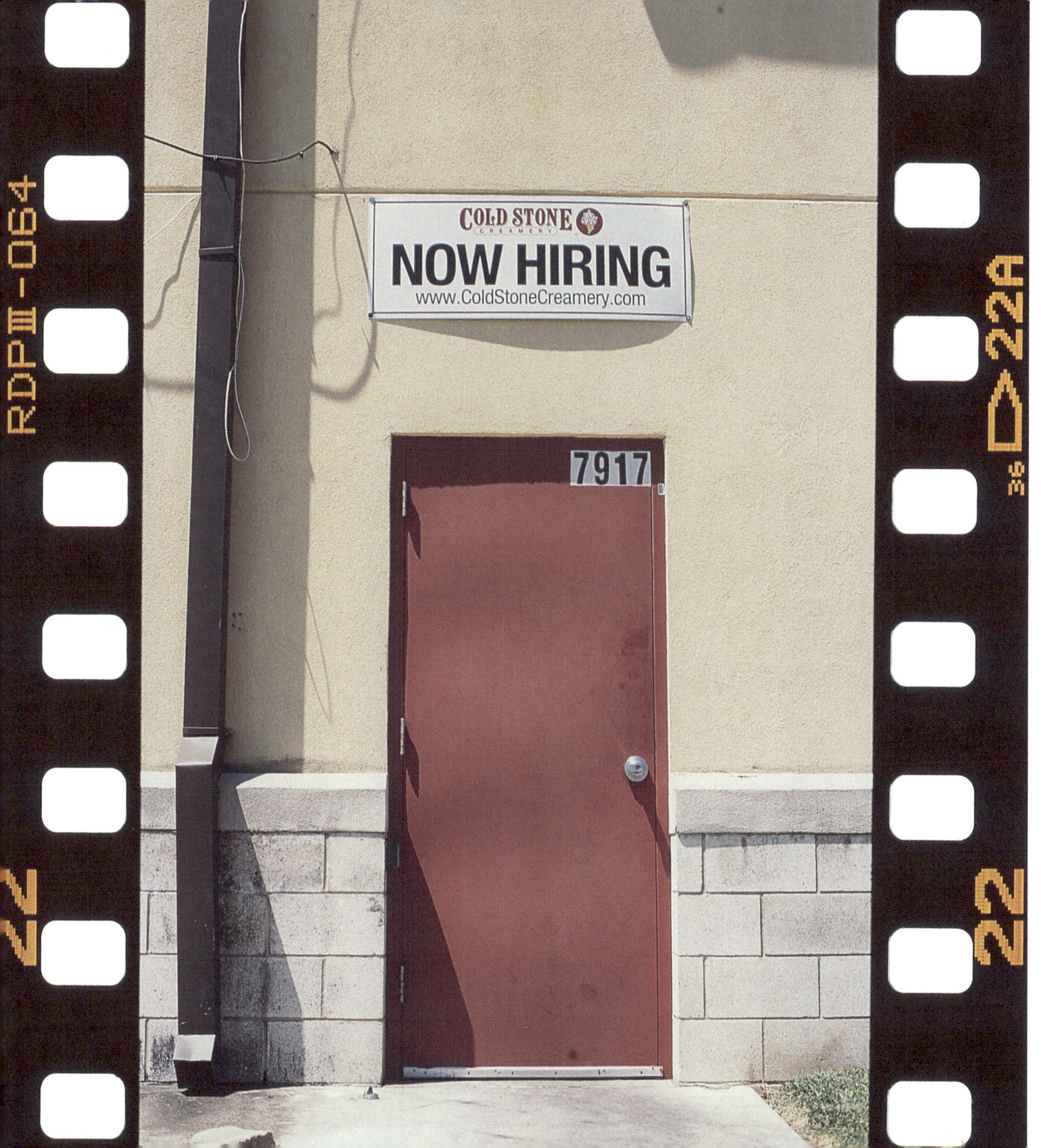

COLD STONE
CREAMERY
NOW HIRING
www.ColdStoneCreamery.com
7917

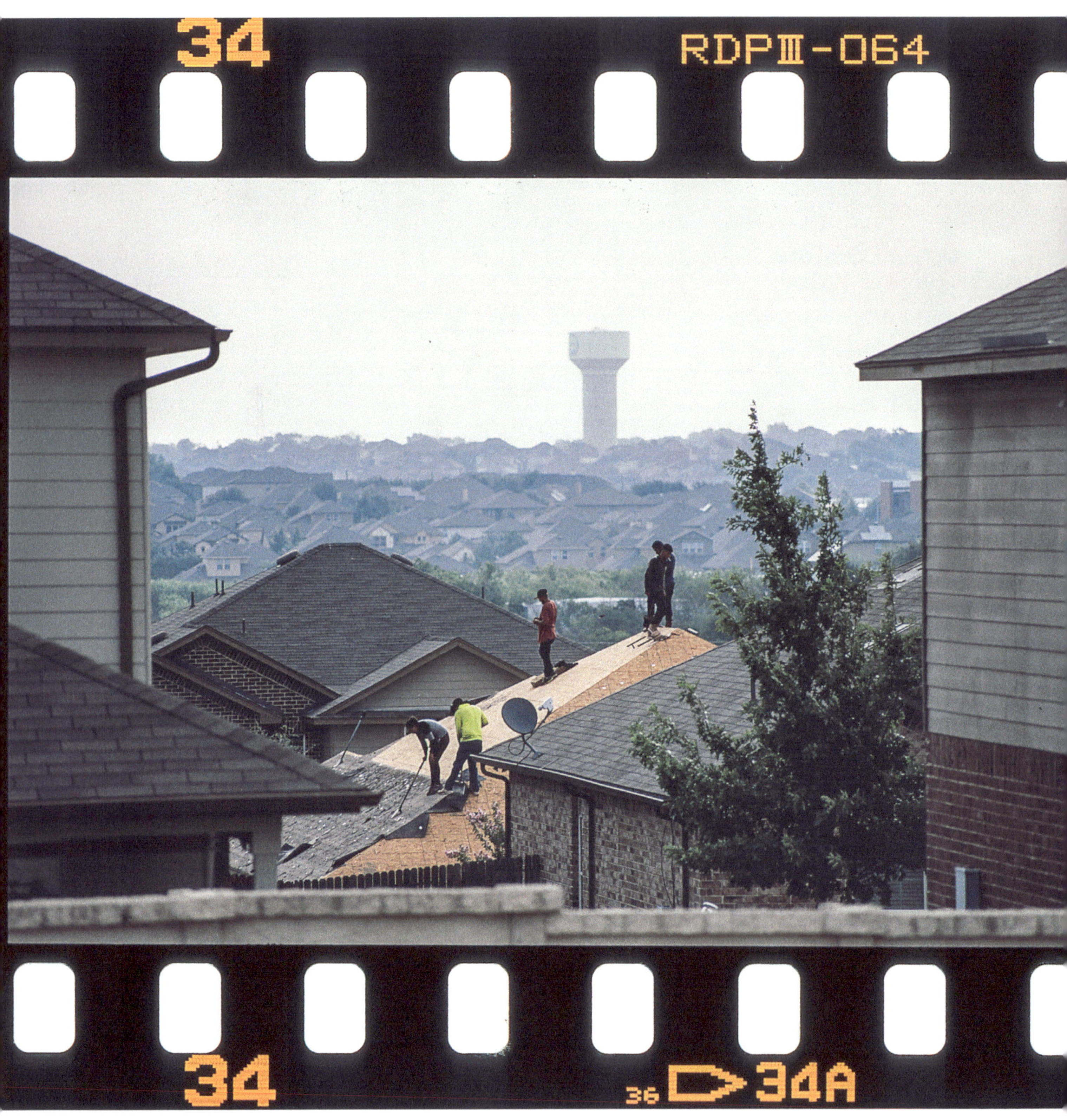
34
RDPⅢ-064
34
36 34A

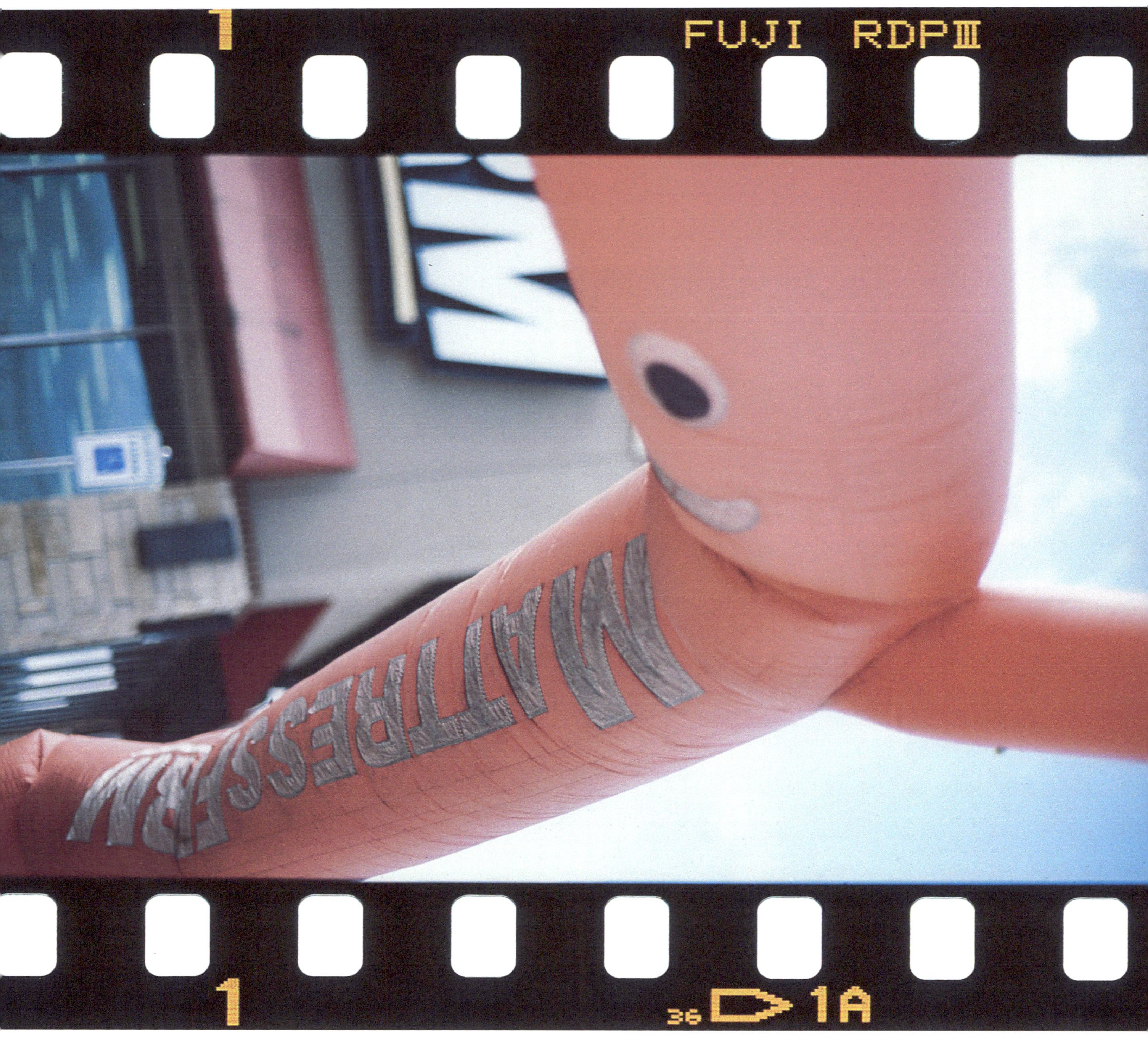
FUJI RDPⅢ
1
36 ▷ 1A
MATTRESS FIRM
M

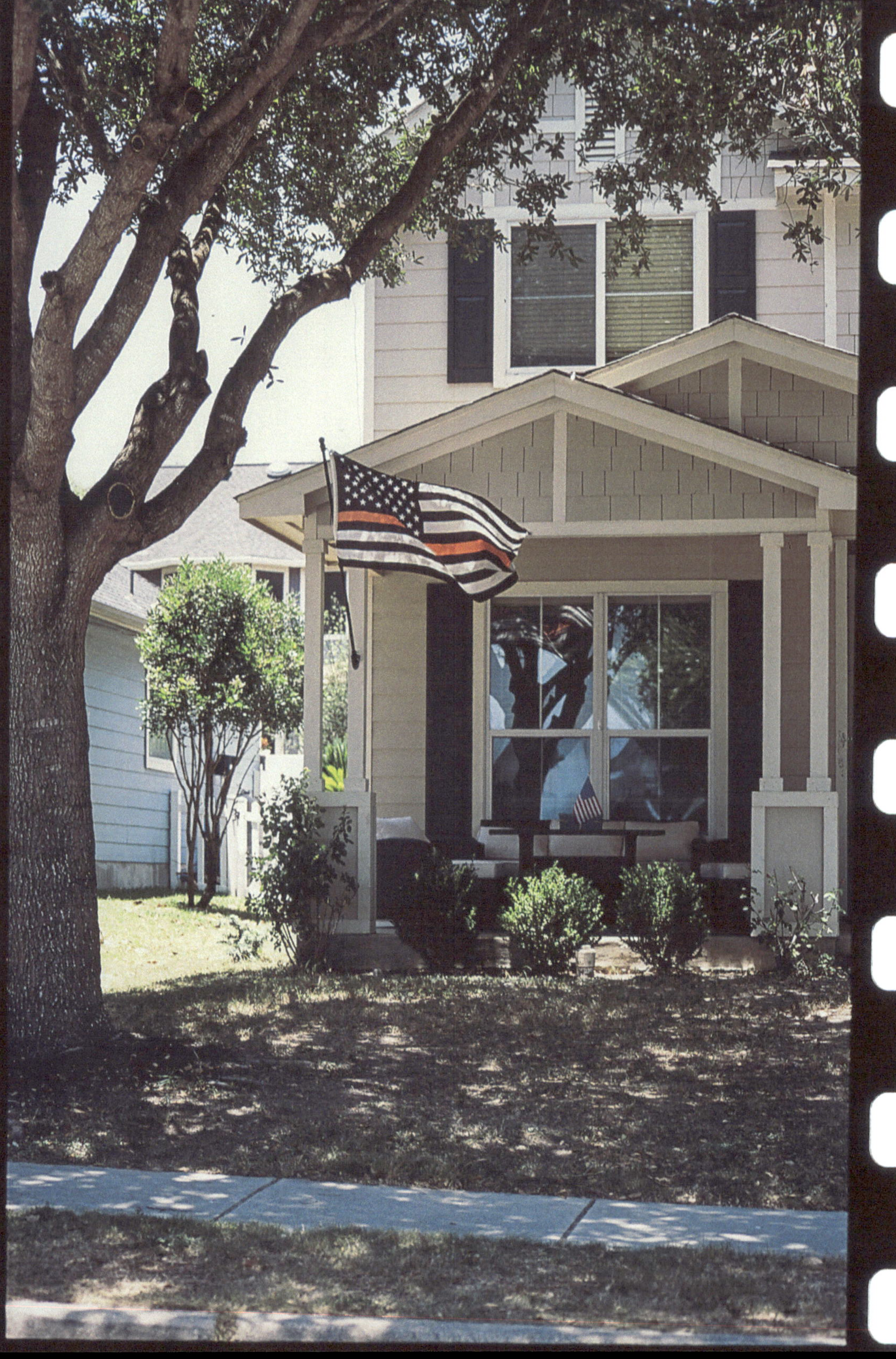

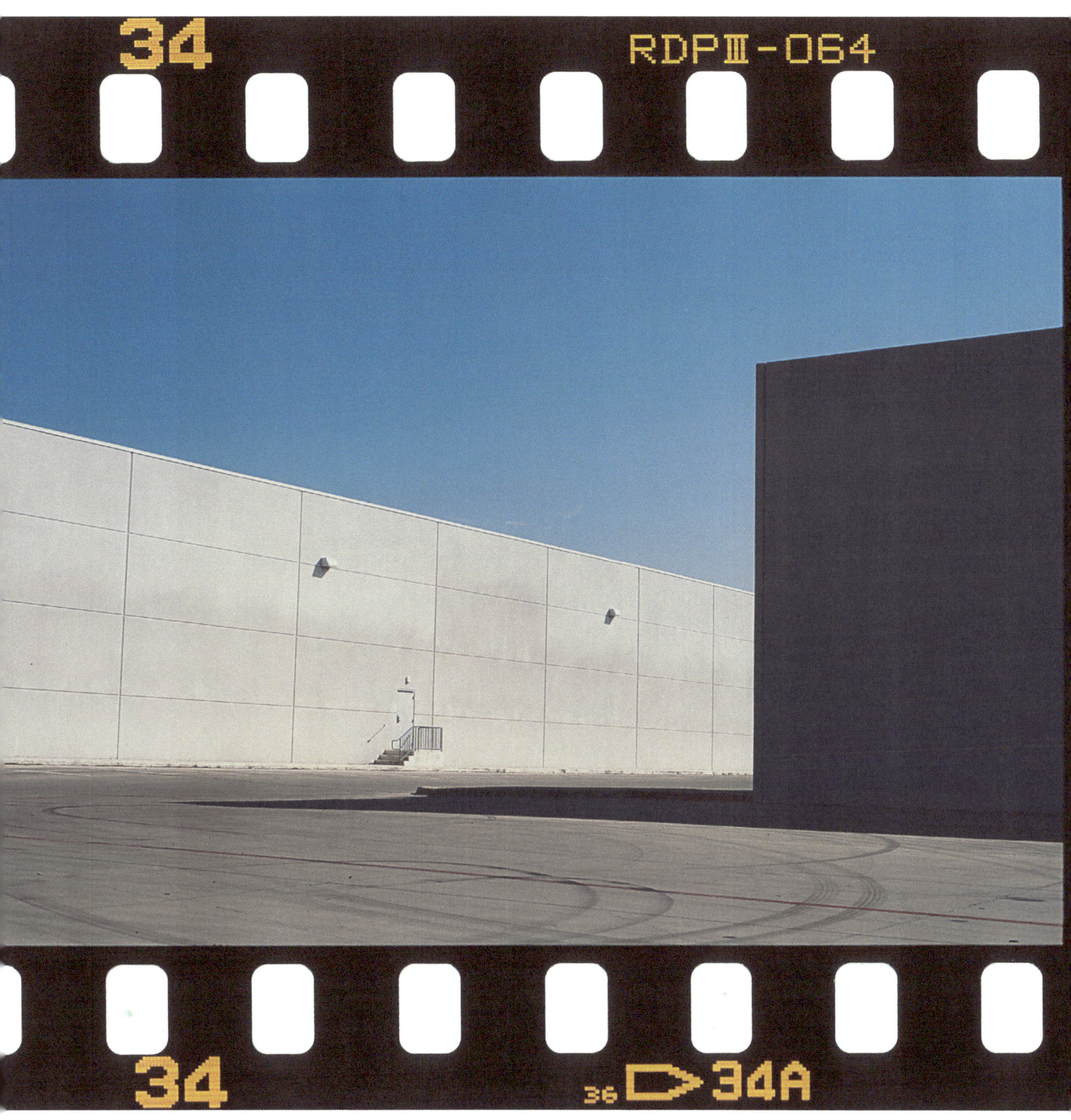
34
RDPIII-064
34
36 34A

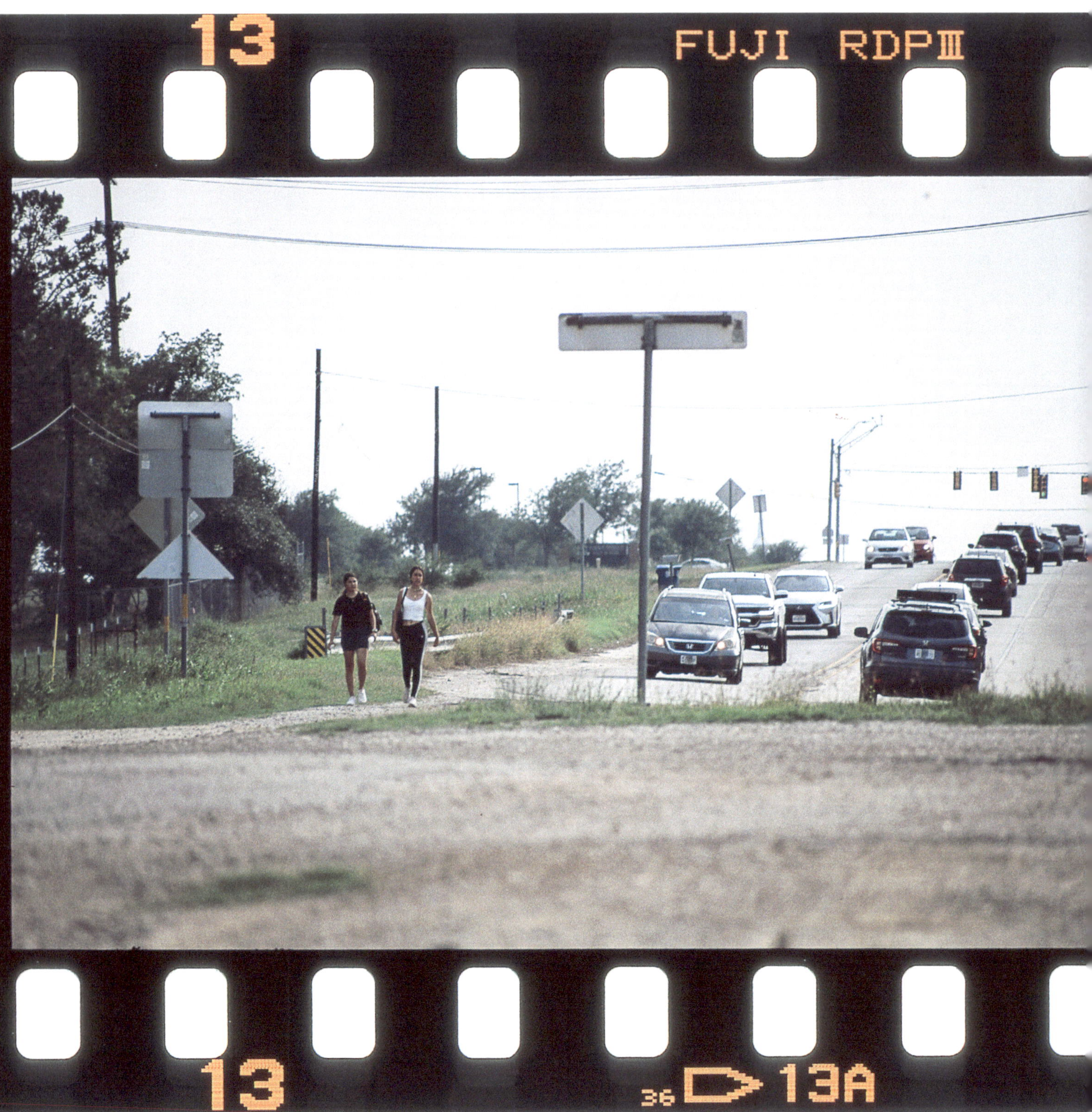
13
FUJI RDPⅢ
13
36
13A

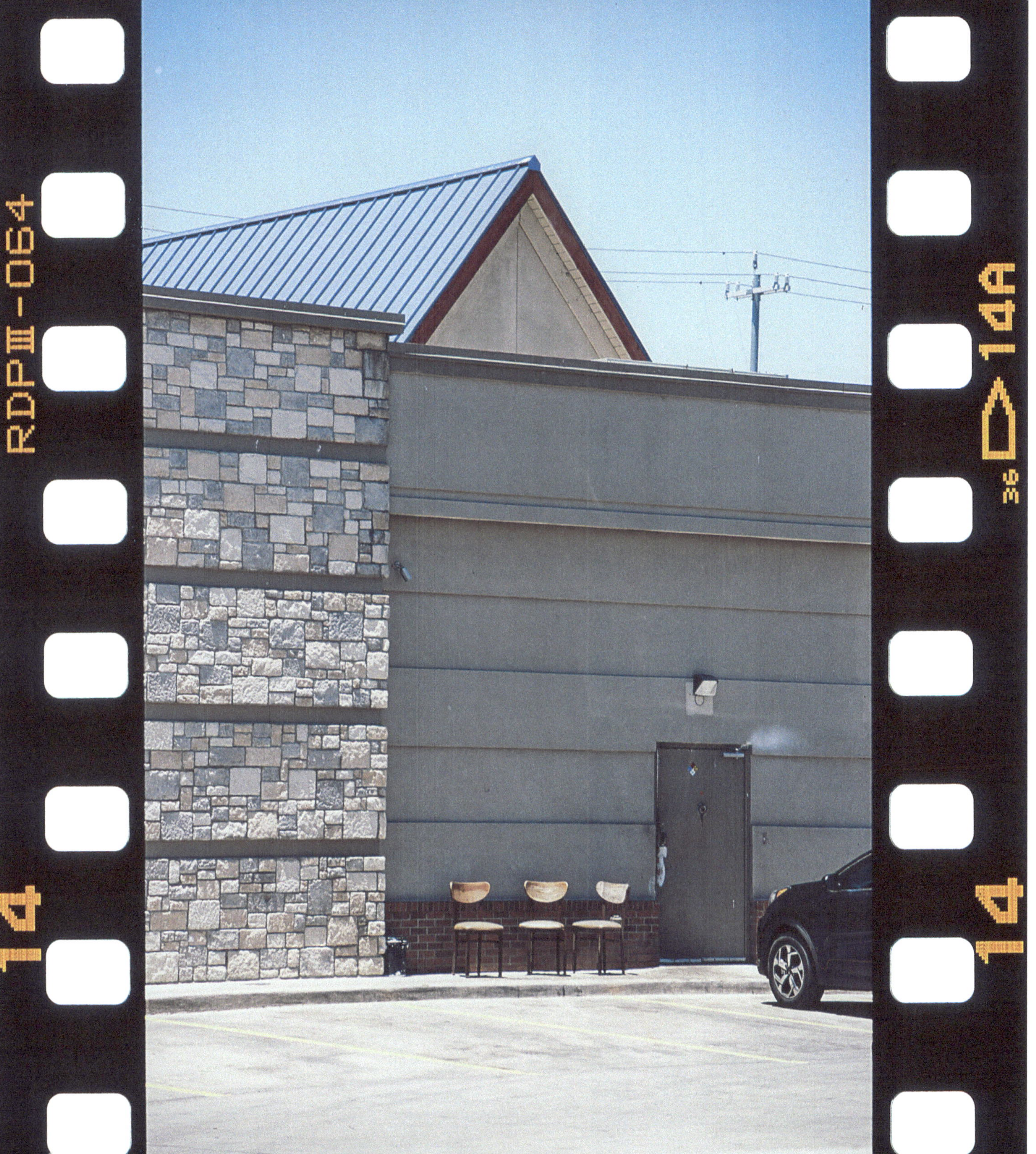